Collins *gem*

5-minute
NLP

D0785603

Carolyn Boyes

First published in 2008 by Collins,
an imprint of HarperCollins
Publishers Ltd.
77-85 Fulham Palace Road
London W6 8JB

www.collins.co.uk
Collins is a registered trademark of
HarperCollins Publishers Ltd.

Text © Carolyn Boyes 2008

8 7 6 5 4
11 10

A catalogue record for this book is
available from the British Library.

ISBN 978-0-00-726659-3

Collins uses papers that are natural,
renewable and recyclable
products made from wood grown
in sustainable forests. The
manufacturing processes conform
to the environmental regulations
of the country of origin.

Edited by Grapevine Publishing
Services
Designed by Judith Ash
Printed in China by
South China Printing Co. Ltd

CONTENTS

INTRODUCTION

Neuro-Linguistic Programming (NLP) is a way of thinking about how the world works, and analysing how excellence is and can be achieved in everyday life. This book explains what NLP has to offer and how you can use it to help you, whatever stage you are at in life, whatever your goal may be.

Why read this book?

NLP offers you techniques to create new results. Perhaps you would like to be a better communicator, enjoy smoother relationships, a better social life or greater career success, earn more money, rid yourself of a habit or phobia, or just know yourself better. Perhaps you are successful in conventional terms but there are still things you would like to change within yourself. You can use NLP to coach yourself, so that you feel happier and more fulfilled. In business, you can use NLP to coach your colleagues, for sales, for presentations and for improved communication and management.

How does NLP work?

NLP is concerned with how the top people in any field consistently achieve results. It is more than this, however – it provides a series of practical techniques that can be learned and applied to all areas of life.

The belief behind NLP is that each person who achieves outstanding results has his own method, process and structure. NLP analyses his thinking and behaviour to make a 'model' of excellence that anybody can copy. Next, NLP shows you how to use this model to replicate the successful methods, and create your own successes. NLP can help you to make use of your inner potential, create a vision and purpose, set effective goals and achieve them.

How to use this book

This book, a pocket edition of *Need to Know NLP* is for anyone who wants to learn about NLP. First, it explains the basic principles, then it looks at techniques for removing barriers and moving towards success. There are exercises throughout the book designed to help you put NLP techniques into practice.

The aim of the book is that you will be able to use your new skills to improve your life. You can begin to use these skills straight away. They are all tried, tested and highly practical. The more you are able to practise them, the better. Try to do the exercises as you go through the book, since you will find this helps your understanding grow. Most importantly, NLP is about experimenting and enjoying new things, so have fun!

THE BASICS OF NLP

In essence, NLP consists of a methodology and a series of techniques for achieving excellence in day to day life. Its structure comes from 'modelling' people who are successful in many different areas. NLP teaches that it is not what happens to you that makes a difference, but what you do with it.

The term 'Neuro-Linguistic Programming' refers to the unconscious processes we use to produce behaviour – and therefore results.

Each component of the name is important:
Neuro refers to the nervous system. Our experience of the world enters the brain via the nervous system and the five senses:

> ✓ visual – seeing
> ✓ auditory – hearing
> ✓ kinaesthetic – touch
> ✓ olfactory – smell
> ✓ gustatory – taste.

One of the first things that NLP is concerned with is how we process this sensory experience and translate it into conscious and unconscious thought.

Linguistic refers to language, specifically the way we use language to give meaning to experience. You communicate your unconscious and conscious thoughts both verbally and non-verbally.

Programming indicates the ways in which we consistently think or behave. Just like a computer, each of us runs specific programmes to produce our behaviour. Programmes consist of a series of steps that automatically produce certain results in different circumstances. NLP can reveal the programmes you run and the results they produce. It also gives you the means to change your own and other people's programmes to produce the results you want.

At the heart of NLP is the belief that anyone can achieve success by learning how other people get their results. This is called 'modelling'.

Modelling
To model someone, you identify a person who does something excellently and you observe how he does it, specifically by looking at, questioning and analysing him to discover:
- that person's language, i.e. the words he uses and the structure of his language
- his physiology, i.e. how he uses his body

- his thinking, beliefs and values, unconscious and conscious.

By copying what that person does in these three areas, you can also achieve excellent results. NLP has an efficient toolkit of techniques to help you do this.

THE HISTORY OF NLP

Given the technical-sounding name, it is not surprising that Neuro-Linguistic Programming was invented by two academics: John Grinder, an assistant professor of linguistics at the University of Santa Cruz, California, and Richard Bandler, who had studied a range of subjects from Gestalt therapy to maths and computing.

Bandler and Grinder drew on existing concepts and ways of thinking to see what they could learn about how people became effective. Grinder was already experienced in modelling, having learned several languages by this method. The 'neuro linguistic' element came from Alfred Korsybski, 'thinker' and founder/author of General Semantics. Another influence was British anthropologist Gregory Bateson. He proposed that there was no such thing as reality, but rather each person unconsciously edited his perceptions of the world to fit his own beliefs. Bateson therefore decided that if people could change their beliefs, they could produce different patterns of beviour.

The models for NLP

Grinder and Bandler modelled three successful therapists, seeking to discover the difference that made the difference – what it was that set these people apart from the average. What was different about their thinking and the way they behaved? How did this produce such successful results?

The therapists they looked at were Milton Erickson, Virginia Satir and Fritz Perls.

Milton Erickson (1901–80) was a psychiatrist and became a highly successful hypnotherapist. The way in which he used language and hypnosis has become known as 'Ericksonian hypnosis'. NLP has modelled Erickson's language to produce the Milton Model (see pp. 100-13) of language patterns. These can be used to put another person into a light 'trance' – a useful state in which NLP techniques can produce change.

Virginia Satir (1916–88) was a family therapist who developed a novel approach based on the idea that there are five key personality areas in people's behaviour (now known as 'Satir categories'). Many of her ideas have become common currency since her death.

Fritz Perls (1893–1970) is known as the founder of Gestalt Therapy, which he co-developed into a general therapeutic tool. He moved away from the psychoanalytical model in which the past is analysed and instead looked at what was happening in the present as the key to change.

Out of the models that Bandler and Grinder produced came a series of techniques that form the strategies that can be used to change behaviour; you will find them outlined in this book.

THE JOURNEY TO WHAT YOU DESIRE

Change is a journey between where you are and where you will be. NLP expresses this as the journey between the present state and the desired state.

If you do not have what you want in your life, it is because the path is blocked by an issue or problem – perhaps a habit you want to change. NLP uncovers the programmes you are running and helps you reprogramme your unconscious mind to change that behaviour.

The instruction to change comes from your conscious mind, but it is the unconscious mind that learns the new way of doing things and produces new behaviour. The unconscious is the same as the subconscious, but NLP practitioners tend to use the former term.

The unconscious mind is everything that is not part of your conscious awareness – it is the home of your beliefs, motivations and behaviour. It acts in habitual, repeated ways. It is your unconscious mind that carries out an instruction from the conscious mind. For example, imagine sitting down – it is your unconscious that tells your limbs what to do.

Four stages
1. Unconscious incompetence
When you begin something new, you don't know what you don't know. If you were learning to drive, for example, you would have no notion of what it would be like if you were able to drive.

2. Conscious incompetence
You are now aware that you don't know. You try to drive and realize how much there is to learn.

3. Conscious competence

By this stage you are relatively competent but your skills are conscious, not yet an unconscious habit. Progress is probably slower, since there is less to learn and it may be more difficult. Your skills are not yet automatic – new drivers still have to think about each thing they do.

4. Unconscious competence (mastery)

You have mastery of your skill. Driving has become a habit. You can drive without thinking about everything you do. The beliefs you have acquired are also unconscious – you simply believe that you are a driver. It has become part of your identity.

THE FOUR RULES FOR SUCCESS

As NLP developed, a set of four rules has evolved that are sound principles for achieving success in any area of your life: know what you want, take action to get it, be flexible and be aware.

1. Know what you want

NLP is outcome-oriented. It always starts with the final goal in mind because its core belief is that you will get whatever you focus on in life. If you don't know what you want, you are essentially acting like a rower without oars – your final destination will not be a place of your own choosing. Many people are not specific enough about their goals. They may know what they want in a very general way, or may just have an awareness of what they *don't* want. It is only if you think through what you want in a specific way that you will achieve very clear and precisely targeted results. (See pp. 76-87.)

2. Take action to get it

People who get the results they want do so by taking action. They may not always have a complete plan, but they can start the journey because they have an end in mind.

3. Be flexible

If you are on track to your goals, keep doing what you are doing. However, if you don't seem to be getting the results you want, in turn try something different. If that doesn't work, try something else. As long as you always keep the result you want in mind and are infinitely flexible in your behaviour, then eventually you will find the right methods to use to achieve your desired result. Be tenacious.

The process of modelling will help you to be flexible (see pp. 180-1). A model of success in any behaviour will provide a very clear example of the ways in which you need to change to get the result you want.

4. Be aware

To be flexible, you need 'sensory acuity' – which basically means being aware in every situation.

5-minute exercise: awareness
• What results are you getting from the action you are taking?
• Are they effective?
• Is there something that you need to change?
These questions will help to steer you in the right direction to achieve your outcome.

EMPOWERING BELIEFS

The empowering beliefs of NLP are known as 'presuppositions'. If you *presuppose* that they are true, you will find that they are helpful for achieving change.

1. A map is only a map

Every person has his own view, or map, of the world. This map is not the same as the territory it outlines – that is, it is not objective truth. What you believe is true is just your perception of the world. If you start to believe that your map is objective reality, it will make you inflexible and resistant to change.

Perceptions, however, are flexible and can be changed. By changing how you see the world (your map), you can orient yourself towards your outcome. NLP contains the toolkit by which you can change your map.

2. Have respect for different models of the world

Because everybody has a unique model or map, other people see the same experience through different eyes. They have different ways of thinking and beliefs from you, and they value different things in life.

The quality of your relationships with others is based on how much you respect these differences. Respect allows you to bridge the gap between your way of thinking and the other person's, and to communicate effectively with them. Being effective in your communication makes you effective in your life.

3. What you do is not the same as who you are

This is a key NLP principle. We often confuse someone's behaviour with who he is as a person.

4. People work perfectly

Everything you have in your life right now exists because you are *already* excellent at getting results – the programmes you run are *all* effective. Your unconscious mind works perfectly, given the instructions it has. If you are not getting the results you want, change the instructions by setting a new outcome. You will have made the best choice you can using your *current* personal resources.

5. We all have all the resources we need

We can all change our beliefs, goals and motivation. So we already have the basic resources necessary to make the change we want. All we need is an attitude of flexibility and a willingness to experiment and learn new skills. In NLP thinking, *there are no unresourceful people, only unresourceful states* – states in which you don't use or don't know how to access your resources. Being unresourceful is a way of behaving, not your identity. Because most of your resources are unconscious, you need to learn to communicate with your unconscious mind to harness them. You can do this using NLP techniques.

6. Underlying every act is a positive intention

The unconscious works for our benefit, and everything it does has a positive intention. So when you observe yourself or someone else behaving in an unconstructive way, you should look for the positive intent behind the action. For example, being rude might have the positive intention of feeling honest.

behaviour

↑

positive intention

7. What you get is what you communicate

Have you ever talked to someone and found out later they misunderstood your meaning? Have you ever been unable to persuade someone, although your case seemed convincing? Has someone ever said one thing to you but seemed to imply another?

Dialogue is a process of feedback from one person to another about what each thinks the other is saying. You cannot *not communicate* – you are always communicating. Even before you say anything, you are sending out messages non-verbally.

In NLP, you can learn techniques to understand how the verbal and non-verbal response you elicit tells you how you are being interpreted. This will enable you to change the way you communicate to ensure that other people receive your intended message.

8. Rapport determines your success in communicating with another person

When you are in deep rapport with someone, you will feel so aligned with his way of thinking that you believe that what he wants must also be good for you – you feel it will also be in your interest. The deeper your rapport with him, the greater your ability will be to influence him. If he resists your suggestions, then your rapport is not deep enough. It is no good trying to coerce or manipulate him. It won't work. To combat resistance, you will need to learn how to deepen your rapport with him.

9. Being flexible ensures the highest chance of success

The more you are willing to play and experiment, the more likely you will be able to establish rapport with those who think very differently from you. Those who can be most flexible in both thinking and behaviour will be most influential. If you keep doing what you have always done, you will always get the same results. If you change what you do, people's reactions will change and your own response will be different.

NLP FRAMEWORKS

The basic ways of thinking about the actions you take are sometimes referred to in NLP as 'behavioural frames'.

Outcome versus blame

Some therapies will look to a person's past to find out why they are not achieving their goals, therefore focusing on the problem (and thus sometimes referred to as the **'blame frame'**). If you use the blame frame to tackle an issue, you are likely to end up asking why a lot: 'Why am I like this?'; 'Why do I do this?' 'Why do I create these sorts of problems?' The implication is that someone is to blame.

Outcome orientation is sometimes referred to as the **'outcome frame'**. NLP is interested in outcomes, not in *why*. It is interested in *how*. It doesn't matter what you do. It does matter *how* you do it. If you know why you do something, you can probably find a justification to continue doing it. If you know how you do something, you can change it.

How versus why

This frame uncovers *how* you do what you do:
- *How* do I do what I do now?
- *What* can I do differently to achieve a different outcome?

Curiosity and experimentation

Adopting curiosity as an attitude will lead you to ask questions. 'How do they do that?' 'What is it that makes that person I would like to emulate so effective?' 'How could I do that too?' You might discover an effective way of doing things as a result.

Experimentation means that you are willing to try new behaviours and apply what you find out. You will learn what results you get from doing one thing rather than another.

Many of us simply *assume* we know what result we are going to get in a given context. If you always prejudge a situation, you are not likely to experiment. Rather, have outcomes instead of assumptions.

Curiosity and experimentation *increase choice*. They were part of your behaviour when you were a child and you had an open mind towards the world. When you want to know more and try new things, you are more likely to succeed, as more choices of action will be open to you.

Feedback versus failure

NLP is focused on *results*. If what you are doing is not working for you it doesn't mean you have failed. You have achieved results – just different ones from those you set out to achieve.

In NLP, everything that happens to us is information we can learn from. So take whatever happens to you as feedback on how near you are to the outcome you want. Life is full of setbacks. The key is whether you view them as opportunities to get new results or as failures.

Believing you can fail will probably lead you to experience negative emotions about yourself if you don't get what you want. These will then stop you from taking further action.

> belief in failure
> = lack of choice/being stuck

> belief in feedback=learning
> new choices, action then results

People who get hung up on the idea of failure are likely to beat themselves up for not getting the result straight away, which means they don't learn what they need to learn to change their actions. Then the whole process of moving forward becomes a struggle. All in all, it is not a very useful belief to hold.

Belief in experience as *feedback* leads to an attitude of flexibility and the likelihood of more positive emotions. If you appear to be a long way away from your goal, simply be flexible and do something else – anything else. Feedback means that you have an opportunity to learn from your experience and to create a clearer path towards what you do want.

Possibility versus necessity

In NLP, it is useful to assume that there are always choices available. Assuming that something 'has to' or 'should' be done limits choice and flexibility. Looking for choices and possibilities makes you the *cause* rather than the *effect* of any situation.

For every event that takes place we can assume that there is a cause, i.e. something created the effect. If we believe that we are affected by causes outside our control, we will not take responsibility for the results we create. We become victims of fate.

NLP calls this 'at effect'.

You'll recognize people who are at *effect* by their language:

• 'I am fat because I have a slow metabolism. There's nothing I can do about it.'
• 'There are no jobs around for people my age.'
• 'Men/women are all confused now, that's why I can't stay in a relationship. They don't want a proper relationship.'

These sentences all place the person as the victim of happenstance.

If you decide to be *at cause* of whatever happens, you switch your thinking around and assume that you can influence what happens next.

For example:

• 'My metabolism is slow but I can change it through exercise.'
• 'Many employers don't want people my age but I will find the exception to the rule.'
• 'What sort of person does want a relationship? How can I attract that person?'

To change your thinking, ask yourself: '*What can I do differently to get the result I want?*'

YOUR INTERNAL WORLD

We each have an individual map of reality (see p. 14), our unique view which determines how we see the world. This is what gives us our life experience. This section explores what goes on in your internal world.

COMMUNICATION

Everyone has a unique set of rules or filters governing how he interacts with people, talks to himself and chooses what to focus on. In NLP this is described as the 'communication model'.

Every second you are bombarded with around two million bits of information. If you were consciously aware of all this, it would be too much to cope with, so you have to filter some of it out.

Your unique set of unconscious filters enables you to make sense of the information coming in from the outside world. They include your beliefs, memories and values.

Your filters change over time and so your map of reality changes too. The information that passes from the external world through your filters is held as an 'internal representation' made up of pictures, feelings, sounds, smells and tastes.

Your internal world determines:
• your state – your particular mindset and emotions
  (the way you feel at any moment; controlling this is
  essential if you want to change your life)
• your body language (in NLP terms physiology)
• your behaviour – the actions you take.

All these are interrelated. The state you are in affects
your behaviour. The internal representations you have
affect your state and physiology. Your state, behaviour
and physiology determine how you experience life at
any moment.

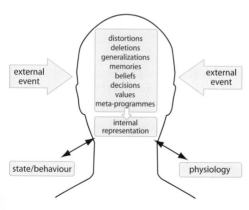

By changing any of these, you can change how you live life.

DELETION, GENERALIZATION AND DISTORTION

You experience the outside world through the five senses: seeing, hearing, feeling, taste and smell. Because they receive so much information, you have to screen out most of the data for your own efficiency and survival. Let's look at how that happens.

Deletion

Every second you delete sensory information from your conscious awareness. Everything that is deleted falls out of your conscious awareness.

What you focus on in life is what you get. When you decide you want something different, you can change what you are focusing on and what you delete. This will give you different results.

If you are helping another person who has an issue that he wants to resolve, it is very important to uncover what has been deleted. Making conscious what you habitually delete opens up new options and the possibility of change.

> **EXAMPLE:**
> Someone tells you about an item of clothing that is currently fashionable. Until they mentioned it, you wouldn't have paid attention to it. You would just have filtered it out. The things you have deleted from your mind have always been there – you simply hadn't noticed.

Generalization

When you generalize, you label information and slot it into categories so that your conscious mind doesn't have to cope with too much difference. This ability can be useful: scientists, mathematicians and artists all use it. Children learn and develop their skills through this technique so that they do not have to cope with too much difference.

If you could not categorize, you would have to invent a new word for every object or experience you had.

But generalizing can be limiting too, making you rigid in your thinking and unprepared to notice exceptions to the rules. You eliminate choice and opportunity by assuming that a past experience will be repeated in the future ('I was hurt in that relationship therefore all future relationships will make me unhappy.')

To combat this tendency begin to pay attention to the exceptions to the rule. Once you begin to realize how much you generalize, you can see the patterns in what you do and notice new information which in the past you might have overlooked.

EXAMPLE:

Imagine you see an animal in the road that looks a lot like a cat. Your brain runs other categories as an alternative: 'Could it be a wild cat, a lion or a tiger? No, it doesn't seem as big as the cats in that category and it seems too friendly. So I am putting it in my domestic cat category.' There it stays until it does something quite uncat-like, such as bark – at which point you have to reassess the broad conclusion you drew about it earlier!

Distortion

Distortion is like putting the wrong lens on a camera – for example, on a day-to-day level, someone says something to you and you distort it in your mind and remember having heard something different from what they actually said.

Distortion is a positive and necessary part of any creative or artistic process. But there is a downside – for example, a man sees his friend talking to his girlfriend and jumps too readily to a conclusion that has a negative implication. He distorts the situation so that he thinks they 'look guilty' and therefore 'must have something to hide' and 'must be having an affair'. In fact, the friend was asking the girlfriend for tips on where to buy the man a present.

EXAMPLE:

Imagine you are alone in a strange house. Every house has its own sounds – creaking, pipes squeaking, noises outside. In your own house, you delete these sounds because you are so used to them. But in a strange house you may focus on them and even begin to distort them. Is that a burglar? Is that a creak of a floorboard or someone talking?

Piecing it together

The filter processes of deletion, generalization and distortion all happen within a matter of seconds, and are unconscious.

To get an idea how this might work, let's take a look at how one piece of information passes through all three filters. Here's a story:

You see your boss smiling at your managing director. He notices you and says, 'I can offer you promotion and better pay.' This seems like great news, but then you remember – the last person he promoted had to make a whole sub-office redundant and was then made redundant himself. You distort your boss's smile. Maybe he was gloating? You delete the memory of the positive things your boss has said to you recently (and the fact that the man made redundant had a very different career history from your own). You start generalizing: isn't it true that all the opportunities you have had in your career have always gone wrong? Won't this be the same?

You begin to use other information to distort your situation: recently the economy has turned down, and there have been job losses. That hadn't bothered you until two of your friends lost their jobs last month. You file the experience to fit: 'You can't trust employers – they're out for what they can get.' You have just been offered promotion and a rise in salary and yet now you feel bitter and cynical!

Listen to your language

Begin to notice deletions, generalizations and distortions by listening to your language. The words you use can give you vital clues. If you hear yourself using phrases like 'I've seen this before', and words like 'everyone', 'people', 'always' and 'never', you could be generalizing. Ask yourself, 'How is it different this time?' The Meta Model (see pp. 92-100) lists questions to use to find out how others are deleting, distorting or generalizing.

Focus on positive pictures

'Don't think of a green bus.' What happens? You think of a green bus.

You cannot *not* think of something that you don't want to think about – you always think about it first!

Pay attention to the pictures you are really making inside your mind. Every time you say 'I don't want a green bus in my life any more', you are making an IR of a green bus and your behaviour and state will be determined by that picture of the green bus you don't want.

If you want to change your life, how about thinking about what colour you really want in your life?

REPRESENTATIONAL SYSTEMS

One of the ways we process information is by choosing to pay more attention to information that comes through one sense rather than another. The experience we have of the outside world through our senses is presented *internally* as images. For example, you can make an internal visual image, an internal sound or a feeling. The means by which we do this are called *representational systems*.

Memories and constructed images

Information received through the senses can be divided into memories and constructed images (imaginings). Both will be represented internally.

THE REPRESENTATIONAL SYSTEMS ARE:

✓ Sight – visual

✓ Hearing – auditory

✓ Feeling – kinaesthetic (this includes your emotions, the feelings inside your body and your sense of touch)

✓ Smell – olfactory

✓ Taste – gustatory

Your preferred representational system

People may switch from one representational system to another from moment to moment, but they may have a preferred system within which they make distinctions about the world. For example, if your preferred system is visual you will remember and construct more visual than sound or feeling images. Your preferred representational system also determines what language you use most frequently. So, if you can listen to your language, you can identify your preferred system and will be able to identify that of people you meet. You can learn how to 'speak their language' and deepen relationships.

As well as a preferred system, you will also have a least preferred system. In stressful situations, we tend to revert to our preferred representational system. Because this determines our use of words, if one person is using words from another person's least preferred system, miscommunication can result.

Your lead representational system

This is different from your preferred representational system. While you use your preferred system most of the time, you use your lead system first of all when you want to access information. It could be visual, auditory or kinaesthetic. For example, if you were asked to remember your journey to work today, you might initially access your *feelings* about it, remember what you *saw* or the *sounds* you experienced during the journey.

EYE PATTERNS: ACCESSING CLUES

There is a link between thought patterns and eye movements. To determine what representation system someone is using, as well as listening to that person's language you can observe the direction in which his eyes are moving.

Visual cues

If you look at another person who is imagining or constructing a visual image, you will notice how that person unconsciously moves his eyes up, and to the right.

If you notice him moving his eyes up and to the left, he is remembering a visual image. If he looks straight ahead with eyes unfocused, he is in 'visual defocused', thinking in a series of pictures.

Auditory cues

If someone moves his eyes to the right, he is thinking about how something will sound in the future. If you notice him moving his eyes to the left, he is remembering a sound or something someone said in the past. If he moves his eyes down and to the left, he is talking to himself ('*auditory digital*').

Kinaesthetic cues

If you notice someone looking down and to the right, he will be accessing a feeling or asking himself, 'How do I feel about what I have seen or heard?'

5-minute exercise to determine eye patterns

VISUAL CONSTRUCTED IMAGES
'What will your bathroom look like if you painted it blue?'

VISUAL REMEMBERED IMAGES
'What did your bathroom look like six months ago?'

CONSTRUCTED SOUNDS
'What would your voice sound like if you had a mask over it?'

REMEMBERED SOUNDS
'What did your bathroom look like six months ago?'

KINAESTHETIC
(feelings and bodily sensations)
'What does it feel like when you touch a soft blanket?'

AUDITORY DIGITAL
(internal dialogue)
'Recite a poem to yourself'

THIS IS AS YOU LOOK TO SOMEONE ELSE

To test a person's eye accessing cues, ask them questions that will cause them to construct or remember feelings, sounds and images or internal dialogue

LANGUAGE AND THE SENSES

Different representational systems use different key words, known in NLP as 'predicates'. Predicates are sensory-specific words. They include verbs, adverbs and adjectives.

People habitually use language that goes with their preferred representational systems and least use language that goes with their least preferred system. If you can communicate with someone using his preferred system, it will increase rapport between you.

PREDICATES – WORDS AND PHRASES

Visual representational system

Look, see, show, clear, bright, picture, clarify, vision, highlight, perspective, illustrate, focus, colourful, seems, survey, dark, scene, spotlight, shadow, vivid, foresee, appearance, watch, illusion, shine, dim, reflect, obscure, eye, sparkle, vivid, watch, dark, light; true beyond the shadow of a doubt / bird's eye view / it appears to me / in my mind's eye / a dim view / in light of your argument / in view of what you say / I see / make a scene / get a perspective on it

Auditory representational system

Noise, hear, resonate, deaf, talk, dissonance, harmonize, speak, rhythm, ask, silent, tune, pitch, clear, buzz, click, audible, earful, proclaim, vocal, cry, say, tell, sound, quiet, discuss, whine, growl, melodious, monotonous, remark, sigh, hum, dumb, call; all ears / an earful / in a manner of speaking / clear as a bell / ring a bell / strike a chord / hold your tongue / lend me your ear

Kinaesthetic representational system

Feel, touch, grab, unfeeling, solid, concrete, hit, handle, tackle, pressure, topsy-turvy, hothead, handle, sticky, scrape, grasp, soft, hard, cold, hot, tackle, solid, concrete, contact, push, pull, gentle, sensitive, tickle, warm, smooth, sharp, seize, pressure; pain in the neck / get a hold of / handle on / catch on to / make contact with / lay your cards on the table / slip your mind / start from scratch / turn something around

Self-talk (auditory digital) has its own set of key words: Sense, think, decide, criteria, process, motivate, learn, mention, perceive, consider, change, conceive.

REPRESENTATIONAL SYSTEMS
Visual

People who primarily use the visual sense tend to talk quickly, breathe high in the chest and are often thin and stand up straight. They think by making pictures so will understand better if you show them pictures.

Kinaesthetic

People who prefer the kinaesthetic sense are slow in speech, breathe deeply from low in the stomach, tend to stand closer to others and like to touch people.

Auditory

An auditory preference may be spotted in someone who breathes from the middle of the chest. They learn by listening and find it easy to repeat what was said. Often their voices are melodic, and they enjoy phone conversations, where they are not distracted by other senses (although they are put off by noise).

Auditory digital

In auditory digital (non-sensory specific) mode, the person shows a mixture of the features of all the other systems.

YOUR STATE AND THE WORLD

If someone refers to a person's 'state', they usually mean their emotional condition – their moods, thoughts and feelings.

What is your state right now? Are you happy, sad, angry, exhilarated, upset, depressed, joyous, energized, curious, excited or interested? The state you are in has an immediate effect on your behaviour, the way other people perceive you and the experiences you have as a result. It also affects the way you see the world and the results you get. You will experience the world differently when you are feeling angry from when you are feeling confident.

While you may not be aware that you have any control over how you feel, in fact you can learn to be more consciously in charge of the state you are in at all times. This is because your state is determined by the pictures you make inside your mind (your internal representations) and by how you hold your body. You can learn to change your pictures and posture, and so change your state. NLP has several techniques to help you do this. (See Changing state, pp. 40-6.)

Your state of mind affects how you hold your body: how you walk, how you sit, the angle at which you hold your head or your spine. Think about how you shift your position when you feel sad. How about when you feel happy or angry?

Think about how the two are interconnected. Imagine you had had a terrible day, then you suddenly had a call telling you about something exciting that was about to happen. Or what if you just put some music on and started dancing? Your state would change instantly, without you having to think about it.

Of course, sometimes you feel good and sometimes not so good, and at other times you can move from depression to happiness or from anger to joy. Most of the time, however, you are probably somewhere in between – this is your 'baseline state'. Your baseline state is determined by how you usually see the world.

Changing state

You can change state by changing what you are thinking about. First, change the pictures you make inside, since this in turn affects you outwardly – it changes your physiology and how you behave. And the way you behave changes the results you get.

5-minute exercise: changing your state

Here is a technique for changing the pictures in your head and therefore changing your state:

1. Think of a time in the past when something happened to you that you weren't happy about.
2. Notice how you feel when you think about this experience.
3. Now notice how you are holding your body.
4. Clear the internal picture screen.

5. Now, remember a particular time in the past when you felt happy or super-confident.
6. Notice how you feel as you remember what happened.
7. Now notice how you are holding your body.

It is important to learn how making negative and positive pictures in your mind affects your body and your state.

Change your physiology/change your state
This technique works in reverse too. If you change your body language, it will change how you feel inside. Actors know this, of course. When you watch a film, notice how they shift their bodies to show a change of mood.

This will work in real life, too. You can immediately change your state by shifting your body until you get the right physiology for the state of mind you want to be in. Think about it. You can't be excited if your body is curled up in a sad, depressed shape. Likewise, you

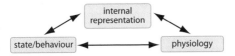

can't be sad if you are jumping around with your hands in the air, head held high and spine straight. You might feel happy, confident or excited, though!

5-minute exercise: changing physiology and state

1. Consider how you would like to feel at the moment (maybe motivated, if you need to get something done, or loving, if you need to talk to a partner or child).

2. Now SHAKE YOUR BODY OUT to lose whatever state you are currently in.

3. Shift your body until you can feel the desired emotion. You can sit, stand upright or move to get into 'state'.

4. Take a deep breath and breathe the way you would if you were in the state.

5. Change your facial expression to match your desired state.

CHOOSING STATES

New states can create new possibilities and bring results. When you feel a little down or demotivated, you are probably slumping or looking down.

But you can change this negative feeling instantly. Stop whatever you are doing. Straighten your spine.

Look up. Put a big smile on your face. Shout out loud, 'Fantastic! Wonderful!' You will feel it too!

Whatever the situation, changing your state from negative to positive will yield results. You won't be able to do a fantastic business presentation if you feel unconfident. You won't make a new friend if you walk into a room looking and feeling angry at the world. However, you will sell something if you feel powerful and positive about selling. And you will make a new friend if you are relaxed and happy and loving.

5-minute exercise: interview states

Imagine you are going for an interview or an important meeting, and are nervous. What would be a useful state to be in? Relaxed? Confident? Cheerful? Happy? Rehearse the scene in your head. Visualize walking into the room, then:

1. State out loud how you would like to feel in positive language ('I would like to feel confident' rather than 'I don't want to be nervous').
2. Now think of a time when you felt this way (if you can't, just imagine what it would be like).
3. Try it on for size to get the memory back (or the imagined feeling in place). Feel it, hear what you heard, see what you saw as if you were there now.

4. You will probably find that you have to adjust your body and expression to get into the right state. Practise in your head and then actually do it on the day. Now you are in a resourceful state, you will be sure to have a successful interview.

Learning state

Have you ever learned something incredibly easily, while at other times it's much harder? That is because learning is linked to the state we are in at the time. Two people might give you the same information, but you will respond differently because of their different states, and the state you are in will also affect how efficiently you absorb that information. If you have ever learned from someone who had no interest in the subject they were teaching you, you'll remember the difference between that experience and learning from someone who was excited or deeply passionate about their subject.

ASSOCIATION AND DISSOCIATION

In NLP, there are two ways of experiencing states – 'association' and 'dissociation'.

Association

When you are 'associated into' a state, you truly experience it – in fact, you often lose your sense of time because you are so absorbed by the experience. Remember something pleasant that happened to you in the past. Imagine that you are actually experiencing now what you did then. See it through your own eyes, feel what you felt and hear what you heard. You can do this with a present event or an imagined (future) event as well.

Dissociation

Dissociation is when you observe an experience. You don't fully experience it – *you think about it rather than feel that you are there in it*. When you remember or imagine an experience, you see a picture of the experience with a picture of you in it. You may still have feelings about the picture, but they will be weaker than you would have if you were associated.

There are times when it is useful to be dissociated – if you want to review an unpleasant memory, or if you need to step outside an experience you are over-associated into in the present.

CHANGING OTHERS' STATES

As well as changing your own state, you can change other people's states as well. If someone else gets into an intense negative state, it is important to be able to help him into a positive state.

If a person is behaving negatively, interrupt their negative behaviour by doing something totally unexpected. This will distract the person and he will dissociate from the state he was in. You can do the same for yourself.

Breaking state is changing from an intense state to a neutral state, giving you the space to adopt another state. You can break state by doing anything that distracts you from your behaviour.

TECHNIQUES TO BREAK OTHERS' STATES

✓ Ask the person to stand up, move around or have a glass of water.

✓ Point to something out of the window or in the room.

✓ Make a noise, or say something that takes his attention away from what he is doing.

✓ Make him laugh.

UNCONSCIOUS FILTERS

Your view of the world is filtered through your beliefs, values, attitudes and memories, as well as a set of deep motivational filters called 'Meta programmes'. You can change these to create new results.

BELIEFS AND BEHAVIOUR

Beliefs are deeply held opinions or views about the world that we perceive to be 'truth', but they are simply our map of how the world is, not the territory. New beliefs are formed as we go through life. They may be changed, discarded or become stronger and more resistant to change. Beliefs determine what you pay attention to. What you pay attention to then guides your behaviour.

Our beliefs are formed unconsciously at different times and from different sources. When you are a child you are exposed to your family's ways of thinking about the world, even if they never talked directly about what they believed. You form new beliefs from any experience that has made you think about life in a different way, and when you encounter new areas of life about which you have no existing opinions.

Most people presume that beliefs and opinions change as a direct result of the information that comes through the senses. In fact, we delete and distort that information according to our beliefs – we only notice the information that proves our existing belief, making it self-fulfilling and resilient to change. In other words, beliefs help to create the reality around us, and you act according to the reality you have created.

EXAMPLE:

Imagine two people who are overweight. One person might say, 'I am overweight because I have a slow metabolism and I am genetically predisposed to this condition.' Because the person believes it to be an absolute truth, he won't make diet and lifestyle changes since he 'knows' whatever he does will be doomed to failure.

The other person may have the same physical problems but believe that he can change his fate because he has seen someone else do it. So he will investigate what foods are unsuitable for him and what kind of exercise will best help him. Because he *believes* he can change, he takes actions.

CORE BELIEFS

'Core beliefs' are beliefs so deeply held that they are essential to our identity and so much part of the way we see the world that we never question them.

EXAMPLE:

A core belief could be an opinion such as 'People are all different.' If you hold this belief, you will look for evidence to reinforce this view. A secondary belief arising from this could be 'People are different, therefore I am different, therefore I can't be as successful as others.' So an opinion that may initially appear to be neutral may in fact limit us enormously.

5-minute exercise: identifying a core belief

1. Stop for a moment and focus on an area of your life.
2. What opinions do you hold about this area? (What do you believe is true about your work? Your relationships? Your friends?)
3. Is it useful for you to believe this?
4. How do you think your beliefs are different from or similar to those of the people in your life?
5. If you were to change a belief, how might that change the actions you currently take in this area?

'Good' and 'bad' beliefs

Beliefs are not 'good', 'bad', 'right' or 'wrong', only 'useful' or 'not useful'. You may have a set of beliefs that work very well for you. However, if your situation changes, they may outlive their usefulness. For example, the belief that you are a kind, considerate person seems likely to produce positive behaviour. Yet it might mean that you forget your own needs, or that you can't make a decision without other people's approval. A new job may require you to make tough personnel decisions that might make you unpopular. How will that fit into your belief about yourself?

NEW BELIEFS ARE FOR AND THROUGHOUT OUR LIVES AND ARE INFLUENCED BY MANY DIFFERENT SOURCES

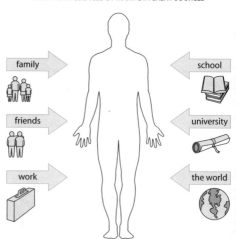

family

school

friends

university

work

the world

Every time you make a decision you change or reinforce a belief. For example, a woman may decide early on in her life that 'all men are bastards'. Later she will have unhappy relationships as she attempts unconsciously to prove herself right.

Sometimes it is simple to change your beliefs – if someone proves to you your opinion is wrong, you will probably change it. However, sometimes you can't change one belief without changing a string of others. In Removing blocks (see pp. 138-59), we will look at how to use specific techniques to change your core beliefs and produce change in your life.

VALUES – THE REASON WHY

Values are another unconscious filter through which we look at the world. Values are what are important to us, what motivates us and gives us a reason why we do what we do. They are the standards by which we live. Love, health, happiness, learning, challenge and relationships can all be values. We may have different values for different areas of our lives.

Your life values are the reason why you choose to live your life in the way you do.
Your relationship values are the reasons why you choose one sort of relationship rather than another.

• Your work values determine why you choose one job rather than another.

Values develop out of our personal experiences, just like beliefs. Some come from the values that your family instilled in you when you were young. Some of your values may become very different from those of your family as you get older. That's because you will also be influenced by other people and experiences: your friends, the media, your education and any different cultures you come into contact with.

THREE KEY VALUES STAGES

It is believed that there are three key ages in life at which we change our values:

1. The imprint period lasts from the moment you are born up until you are seven. At this young age, you soak up values unconsciously from the people you are with most of the time; your family probably.

2. The second stage – the modelling period – is from around the age of 7 to 14. Your world generally gets bigger as you go to school and you are influenced by the wider variety of people you meet and look up to and who may have different values from your family.

3. The third stage – the socialization period – is from around the age of 14 to 21. At this age, we can exercise

much more critical judgement about what we value. We have to choose how we are going to find a place in society and therefore which of our original values we may want to reject or replace. At this stage, you may find yourself in conflict with your friends or family.

Carrot and stick values

We are motivated by two types of values: values that pull us towards something, and values that push us away – carrots to tempt us, sticks to spur us on.

For example, if you want to be rich, this is positively expressed and is a '**towards**' value. However, if you work only because you 'don't want to be poor' rather than because you 'want to be rich', then you are motivated by an '**away from**' value. The unconscious processes by forming pictures, so if it hears the statement 'I don't want to be poor', it first of all forms an internal representation of what it doesn't want – 'poor'.

So, if your value is 'not wanting to be poor' then your internal representation is of 'poor'. Therefore your unconscious keeps filtering for the thing you don't want, the picture of 'poor'. You may find that money keeps on slipping through your fingers.

To make the changes you want in life, you need to get a picture of what you *want* instead of what you *don't want*.

5-minute exercise: values
To discover your values about something ask yourself:
1. 'What is most important to me about X?'
2. 'How do I know when I have X?'
3. 'What is the next most important thing about X?'
4. 'What else is important to me about X?'
The answers you generate are your values.

Extended exercise: life values
Answer the following questions to determine your life values:
1. 'If I were to begin my life right now, what would I want?' 'What is important to me?' 'How do I want to live my life from now on?' 'Why?' 'Who is really important to me?' 'If I could choose how I spent my time, where would I focus my energy?' 'What kind of work and social life do I want?'
2. Review the major events and choices you have made in your life. Think of a time when you did something that seemed and felt totally right (some people use the phrase 'in the flow'). Ask yourself:

'Would I make the same choices again?' If yes:
'What was important about this choice to me?'
If no: 'What was important?' 'What was it about it
that made it right?' 'What was present?' 'What was
absent?'

Alternative extended exercise: key values
Go out into the future several years from now and
look back at yourself in the present time. You
would be able to notice everything you have now
that is really important to you from your vantage
point of the future. Ask yourself: 'What would you
want to have spent your time doing?' 'Who would
you have wanted to spend your time with?' Once
you have identified what is important to you,
imagine if you had to live life without it. If you feel
you could, it is probably not a major value.

MEMORIES

A memory is a stored representation of something
you have experienced. It is your perception of what
happened at the time. Everybody's memory of an
event will be different because it will be distorted,
deleted and generalized according to each person's
model of the world.

Memories also act as filters of our experience in the present. For example, suppose when you were small your parents divorced after a big argument. Later in life you have difficulty in a relationship as soon as there is conflict, because you are afraid that any argument will trigger its end. In fact, there may have been many other factors that caused your parents' divorce, but this memory has been linked in your mind with the idea of break-up.

Take another example. When you were very young you were frightened by a ladybird crawling onto your hand. You still don't like them now, although you no longer have conscious awareness of the incident. The memory, however, still acts as a filter.

With NLP techniques you can address these kinds of limitations on your current behaviour, even if your memories are way back in your childhood. See Removing blocks, pp. 138–59.

META PROGRAMMES

The final set of internal filters we have are known as Meta programmes. These are deep unconscious filters that influence personal and work behaviour. The charts on pages 57–64 will help you to categorize your own Meta programmes.

MOTIVATION

Do you habitually move towards what you want in life, or away from what you don't want? To find out what your habitual way of doing things is, ask yourself the question: 'What do I want out of work?' Is your reply to this question mainly things you want to have or to be at work, or things you want to avoid? Are you mainly:

- ✓ towards
- ✓ away from with some towards
- ✓ towards with some away from
- ✓ away from
- ✓ equally towards and away from

REASON

This looks at whether you are motivated because you feel you have to do something or because it gives you possibilities. Ask yourself these questions to find out which you are: 'Why am I choosing to do what I am doing in my work life? Is it because it gives me choices or possibilities or is it because of a sense of obligation?' Are your answers to this question mainly:

✓ necessity   ✓ possibilities   ✓ a mixture of both

ACTION AND REFLECTION

Are you an active or a reflective person? Active people jump in and get on with things as quickly as possible. They like to get started without spending too much time thinking about what they are doing. At the other end of the scale, reflective people prefer to spend time thinking things through in as much detail as possible before they start.

The questions to ask yourself are: 'If I had a project to do, would I leap in straight away and get started on it? Or would I wait first and think it through before acting?' Decide, are you:

✓ active ✓ reflective ✓ both

FRAME OF REFERENCE

What is your frame of reference for knowing something? Do you just know inside or do you need to have some sort of external check – for example, to talk to someone and ask his opinion? The questions to ask are: 'How do I know whether I have done a good job? Do I just know? Do I need someone to tell me? Is it a mixture of both?' Your answer determines whether you are:

✓ internal check   ✓ external with an internal check
✓ internal with an external check   ✓ external check

RELATIONSHIP FILTER

Each of us has a different way of noticing similarity and difference. Some people notice the similarities between things. Some people notice the differences.

People who notice sameness (people who 'match') like their jobs and relationships to remain the same. They generally are happy to stay in the same job for more than five years before they need to seek out change.

✓ 'Sameness with difference' people like more change – after about three to five years.
✓ 'Difference with exceptions' people need greater variety – after about 18 months to three years.
✓ 'Difference' people ('mismatchers') need a lot of the new in their lives and will seek out change and variety.

Other questions you can ask to find out sameness or difference is: 'How long do I usually stay in a particular work situation?' 'When I start a new relationship, do I notice the differences first or the similarities?'

BIG PICTURE OR SPECIFIC?

Are you a big picture or a detail thinker? Do you enjoy thinking in abstract terms or prefer being specific? Some people have the ability to move from the detailed to the big picture and back again. This amount of flexibility can make you highly successful in the business world, where only being able to be either specific or big picture would be very limiting. The questions you need to ask are: 'If I were working on a new project, how much detail would I need to know? How about when I am describing my vision of the future? Do I talk first about the details or the big picture?' Notice whether you are:

✓ big picture
✓ specific
✓ big picture to specific
✓ specific to big picture

CONVINCER

What does it take to convince you about something? For some of us it takes a number of times of hearing/seeing/doing/reading something. Others may need to have the same evidence in front of them, or different examples relating to the same subject, a number of times. A very common number of times is three, which is why you often see advertisers repeating

BIG PICTURE OR SPECIFIC?

How would you describe what you see through the window?

How do you see the relationship between these stamps?

an advertisement on television more than once in a short time. Alternatively, your convincer might be that you need to see/hear/do/read something over a period of time.

Some people automatically become convinced the first time they see/hear/do/read something. Others will need to have the same data in the same way each time.

They have what is called a 'consistent convincer'. Questions to ask yourself are: 'How long does it take me to become convinced by a choice? How many times?' 'Do I know that I am good at my job automatically? Do I have to be consistently convinced? Does it take a period of time?' Is your convincer:

✓ automatic	✓ a period of weeks
✓ under three times	✓ a period of months
✓ over three times	✓ consistent

THINKING AND FEELING

Do you get caught up in your feelings, or are you able to step back from them? Or does it depend on the circumstances? Questions to ask yourself are: 'When I have been in a situation that I found challenging, was I very affected by it? Did I immediately dissociate from my feelings? Or was it a combination of the two?' Are you:

✓ feeling ✓ thinking ✓ moving between the two

TIME

Have you ever met someone who appeared to be totally unaware of time? Are you like that? You live life so in the moment that you are often very late or very early for appointments. You often don't wear a watch and are reluctant to put too much in your diary too far ahead. This is known as 'being in time'.

Other people are always aware of time; they are punctual and like to have life mapped out in advance. This is called 'being through time'.

Questions to ask are: 'Do I plan my time ahead, even on holiday? Do I like filling up my diary weeks ahead? If I did this, would I feel unable to live in the moment?' Are you:

✓ through time   ✓ in time

PRIMARY INTEREST FILTER

What is your main focus in life, your primary interest? The questions that will determine this are: 'What makes me happy? The people I am spending time with? The things around me? The place I am in? The activities I am doing? The learning/information I am gaining?' Are you interested in:

✓ people   ✓ activities   ✓ things
✓ information/learning   ✓ places

SELF OR OTHERS?

During a typical day, pay attention to what it is you focus on – is it on yourself or on other people? The answer may well determine the type of job you do. People who usually work well in the service industry are likely to have a strong interest in other people. If you prefer to work in an area where you don't have to think about other people's needs, you are more self-oriented. Are you:

✓ self   ✓ others

DECISION-MAKING

Decisions are normally made through a series of steps. You may need to see something before you can make a decision, or hear about it or even do something first. The question to ask is: 'How do I know whether a product is any good?' Do you need to:

✓ see   ✓ hear   ✓ do   ✓ read

FORMING RELATIONSHIPS

If each person has a different perspective on life, then how can you learn to relate effectively with so many different types of people? In this section, you will learn the secrets of building instant rapport with anyone. Rapport is the basis for effective communication and deep relationships.

CONSTANT COMMUNICATION

Communication is a constant flow of information between two people. Whether you are face to face, or at the end of a telephone, you are sending each other messages about who you are and what kind of relationship you want with each other.

The moment you meet somebody he will begin to form an impression of you, whether you are speaking to that person or not. The instant you are aware of each other you are communicating.

Some of our first impressions come through what we hear another person saying, but many more come from what we *see* him doing and what he *looks* like. Along with all our other impressions of the world, our first impressions are filtered through our representational systems.

5-minute exercise: flexible communication

Try reading this statement in different ways. First read it flat. Then let your voice rise at the end of the sentence. Then let your voice go down at the end of the sentence. How does your voice sound?

• 'Fetch me that book' ? (voice flat)
• 'Fetch me that book' ? (voice down)
• 'Fetch me that book' ? (voice up)

The first statement is neutral, the second is a command and the third a question. Yet all that has changed has been your tone.

DID YOU KNOW?

• Only 7% of your communication is verbal – the 'content' of your communication.

• 38% is conveyed though the quality of voice – tone, volume, speed and pitch.

• 55% is through your posture, movements, gestures, facial expressions, breathing and skin-colour changes.*

*Ray L. Birdwhistell, Kinesics and Context, University of Pennsylvania , 1970

RAPPORT

Have you ever walked into a room, met somebody for the first time and decided within seconds that you liked him? You probably didn't think too much about why, you just noticed how easy it was to speak to him. Or maybe you once met somebody you took an instant dislike to? Perhaps he had an over-strong or weak handshake. Maybe he didn't look straight at you when you were speaking. Whatever it was that made you like or dislike a person, it probably happened almost immediately and was unconscious.

It is natural to like people who seem to think like we do. At a party you will probably gravitate to people with whom you have things in common. However, there are charismatic people whom everyone seems to like and who are very good at getting on with a wide variety of people, even if they don't seem to have much in common with them in terms of background or interests.

What is happening here? Rapport. Charismatic people can create a rapport very quickly with almost anyone. You can learn how to do it too.

When you are in rapport with someone it feels as if you are both on the same wavelength – there is integrity, caring and trust. When he talks to you, he feels a sense of comfort and understanding coming from you. Having rapport helps you communicate at a deep level. Because the other person feels you are like him, he is at ease and ready to open up to you.

How can you build rapport?

Start by breaking down your communication into its verbal and non-verbal elements:

1. Words: The words and phrases you use can say a lot about you: your nationality, culture, age, gender and class, interests, values, beliefs and the kind of work you do.

2. Physiology: Your non-verbal communication can reveal your emotions, the power you have in relation to the other person and whether you are sexually attracted to them. Your posture, expressions and gestures all leak information (whether or not you are trying to control them).

3. Voice: The next time someone phones you, pay attention to his voice. People say a lot through tone, speed, pitch and timbre (vocal texture).

CALIBRATION

To notice the effect you are having on the person with whom you are communicating is called 'to calibrate' or 'to have sensory acuity' in NLP. This describes your ability to notice with great precision what is going on around you.

Calibration means non-judgemental observation of the tiny minute-by-minute changes in someone's voice and body.

When you are calibrating another person, be aware that a form of behaviour that means something to you in a certain situation does not always mean the same to someone else. Look for repeated non-verbal clues. Practise calibrating another person using the following exercise.

5-minute exercise: calibration

Sit or stand at a 90 degree angle in relation to the other person so that you can observe what that person is doing with his body. At the same time, you can hear what he is saying (the words and language), as well as listen to his voice characteristics. You will find it is easier to see what is going on at this angle than if you are directly opposite the person. If you are opposite him, it will look as though you are staring at him while you are talking, and this is likely to make him feel uncomfortable – not a good way to build rapport! Observe shifts in the other person's:

1. Breathing: Look for the rate and location. Is it fast or slow? Where is he breathing from? The chest or stomach?

2. Skin colour: What does his skin look like? Has it become lighter or darker? Shiny or non-shiny?

3. Mouth: Sometimes the lower lip size will look bigger or smaller than normal

4. Eyes: How is their focus changing? Are the pupils dilating or expanding?

5. Face: Have the muscles in the face slackened or tightened to make the face look more asymmetrical or symmetrical?

6. Voice: Note any changes in the tone, tempo or sound (timbre) of the voice. Is the person speaking more quickly, slowly, louder, softer, or is the voice clearer or more broken up?

MATCHING

If you have ever seen a pair of close friends or a happy couple in love, you will have noticed that they tend to copy each other's little non-verbal habits and speak the same language – picking up ways of saying words or phrases. They also make a lot of eye contact and their body language is in sync. If one gestures in a particular way when talking, the other will tend to gesture with the same movements when he talks. They are not mimicking each other, but they have unconsciously got into rhythm with each other.

Next time you are in a restaurant, look around you. Which couples or groups of people are in rapport?

When rapport doesn't come automatically, you can build it by matching. Matching another person's communication is the way to build rapport at a deep unconscious level. When two people are in rapport they naturally match or adopt some of each other's words, as well as postures, sometimes gestures and voice tone and speed: you feel connected to each other.

This is not the same as mimicry – when you mimic someone, you copy everything about him (and probably anger him). Matching is more subtle and stays outside the other person's conscious awareness. Be subtle. Get into the rhythm of his voice and body. Be careful therefore about copying someone's gestures too obviously – it can easily become mimicry. Posture is the quickest detail to match.

If you are successful, you will warm to the other person and have a feeling of deep rapport.

5-minute exercise: matching physiology
Observe the other person's sitting or standing position. Match any of the following: posture, facial expressions, gestures, head tilt, breathing – from the chest or the stomach. You can even match someone's blinking rate for a few seconds.

Matching

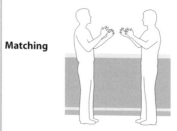

5-minute exercise: matching voice
Voice qualities: You can match a person's voice qualities, words he marks out by tone or emphasis in his sentences, and other linguistic idiosyncrasies such as his sentence length, jargon or particular phrases. Each person has a few words and phrases

that he marks out in his speech by using them time and time again or by putting particular emphasis on them. This is language that has some personal meaning or emotional or cultural significance. Use these words and you will sound like him.

Speed or pace: How people speak varies considerably according to their preferred representational system (see pp. 36-8), mood, culture or nationality. A businessman from the country may talk much more slowly and softly than a businesswoman from a fast-paced city.

Timbre: the quality of the voice. Notice whether his voice is clear and resonant or gravely and harsh. What is your own voice like? Can you change it?

Markers of rapport

As you match the other person, as long as it remains outside his conscious awareness, the two of you will begin to get into rapport.

• You might notice a warm feeling, probably in your stomach.

• Your face and neck may change colour slightly.

• You may suddenly feel close to the other person, as if you have known him for a long time.

Pacing and leading

In NLP, building rapport is known as *pacing and leading*. *Pacing* is when you match the other person, *leading* is when you lead them into another state.

EXAMPLE:

Suppose you are in a good mood. The phone rings, and it is a friend who is frantic because his wallet has just been stolen. How do you keep rapport with him without bringing your own mood down? Match some of his key words or voice qualities. If you try to calm him by using the opposite kind of voice, he is likely to be annoyed because he will feel you haven't *got* what he is saying.

Once you have paced the other person, you have demonstrated you are on his side. You can now start to lead by keeping rapport while gradually changing the speed at which you are talking, or shifting position so that he follows you, so changing his emotional state.

Mismatching

This is when you are not in rapport and are not getting along with each other. You match neither verbal nor non-verbal communication. When you are out of sync you will feel disconnected from the other person.

There are times when you may want to deliberately break rapport and mismatch. In this situation, you can shift your position so that you break the state you are both in. You can do this very quickly and easily just by looking or turning away, or stepping back. The conversation will suddenly shift and you will have the opportunity to end it with merely a few words.

Mismatching

CREATING OUTCOMES

What makes some people more successful than others? What makes a tennis champion or a top business person? Consistent high achievers are outcome-focused – they decide what they want, they are motivated and they take action to get it.

5-minute exercise: what do you want?

Could your life be improved by setting some outcomes? Consider a quick brainstorm:
1. Do you know where you are going?
2. Have you achieved what you want professionally?
3. Do you have the relationships you want?
4. Do you have the friendships you want?
5. Have you achieved a work/life balance?

Unless you have answered yes to all of them, you could probably introduce some more focus and clear outcomes into your life to get what you want.

The first step to anything is to wish for it. The next step is to make your wish into an outcome. An outcome is a clear statement and representation in your mind of what you want.

This will begin the process of focusing your thoughts away from any present dissatisfaction and towards what you want as a final goal.

Do any of these stop you knowing what you want?

- ✓ You think you shouldn't or can't have it.
- ✓ You are used to focusing more on the past or present than the future.
- ✓ You are afraid to voice it.
- ✓ You think you will lose too much in another area by having it.
- ✓ You think it is impossible to get.
- ✓ You are used to thinking about other people's wants rather than your own.

If you answer 'yes' to any of these questions, list your beliefs about yourself and use the belief change techniques described on pp. 143-4 to help free up your thinking.

Outcomes set a direction

An outcome may refer to the result you want to get from taking a specific action, or may be a long-term goal. Either way, it sets a direction for you – an outcome is where you now intend to focus your energies and actions.

Use your outcome as your destination: always start with the destination in mind and plot a journey from your present position to that place.

BIG VISIONS

Highly successful people have one thing in common – inspiring, motivating visions that pull them forward and allow them to overcome any obstacles.

A study at an American university asked first-year undergraduates whether they had written down their goals. Around 5% had. Twenty years later, the same researchers discovered those 5% were worth more than the other 95% put together on a fiscal basis, and held more positions of power and influence in industry, business and government.

YOUR VISION

What is your vision? It will need to be big enough to inspire you and, if necessary, those around you. The secret of success in life is: focus, action, persistence. First you focus, then you take action, and finally you are persistent. Remember: a vision doesn't need to be probable; it just needs to be believable and possible for you to achieve it.

Outcome-based thinking

Thinking in terms of outcomes is known as 'outcome thinking' or 'having an outcome orientation'. Outcome-based thinking asks questions such as: 'What do I want and what steps can I take to get it?'

Problem-based thinking

Focusing on your current problems rather than a vision or outcome is known as 'problem thinking'. This is blame-based and will ask questions such as 'Who's responsible for causing the problem?' Problem-based thinking will keep you stuck in the problem. Outcome-based thinking will move you forward.

Well-formed outcomes

If a general goal is to become a compelling outcome you need to have a sharp and focused image, known as a 'well-formed outcome', of what it will be like when you have achieved it. This will make it motivating enough to make you want to move from your present position (present state) to your outcome (desired state). It will also inspire you to take action and counter any resistance.

An outcome is well-formed if:

✓ It is stated in positive language.
✓ You have stated evidence for how it will look, feel and sound when you have it.
✓ It is specific and set in a context (where and when you want it).
✓ You can do what is necessary to achieve it – you are responsible.
✓ It is good for you and for your life as a whole.

Exercise: clarifying vision and outcomes

To help another person, begin by finding out what his outcomes are. The clearer he is about what he wants, the easier it will be to work out what techniques and tools will create the change he wants.

Here are a few pointers:

1. Clarify what he would like to have achieved by the end of your time together.
2. Discover his overall vision for his future and how the outcomes fit into it. The bigger and more specific the person's vision, the easier it will be to come up with a set of goals with different end dates to support it.
3. Discern which of his outcomes are particularly important to him (he may not state them outright – observe his body language and note emotionally charged words).

OUTCOME QUESTIONS

For each outcome, run through the following questions to ensure it is well formed and easily realizable.

1. What do I want?

Because what you focus on is what you get, make sure you use positive language to state your outcomes, and *write them down*. Positive language does not mean that you have to feel positive when you think of the outcome. It simply means focusing on what you want rather than what you don't want (for example, 'I want a new car' rather than 'I don't want my beaten-up old car.') If you don't, you are likely to end up with what you were trying to avoid.

If your main motivation is to *move away* from a current situation, ask yourself: 'What do I want *instead*?'

Be specific. Imagine you want to go to America. You choose to fly from London, but do not specify a US city. If you ended up in New York or California, would it make a difference? Of course it would. You wouldn't dream of doing that, so treat your outcome as a specific destination too. For example, if you want more money, write down how much you want *specifically*.

Write your outcome in the present tense. Instead of saying, 'My goal is to have an annual salary of £1,000,000 by 20 August 2020,' say 'It is 20 August 2020 and I have an annual salary of £1,000,000.' The brain processes a goal that has been written in the present tense as if it is actually a truth now, so you act accordingly.

2. Where am I now?

To achieve what you want, you need to move from where you are now (your present state) to your outcome (desired state). So when you write down your outcome, note your starting-point as well. You will then be able to monitor how far you have travelled on your journey.

3. How will I know when I have it?

A well-formed outcome needs an evidence procedure, for two reasons:

1. So that you know when you are on track or have gone off track. How will you measure how near you are to it?

2. So that you know you have achieved the outcome. How will you know? What will you hear, see and feel when you have it?

Think about what your experience of getting what you want will be like. For example, when you have a fit, toned, muscular body, what does that feel like? What is it like to earn as much as you wanted to?

Imagine you have what you want. Try it on. What does it feel like inside? What else can you feel, see and hear? What are people around you saying? Does it feel good?

4. Where, when, how and with whom?

There may be some situations in which you desire an outcome and others in which you don't. For example, you might seek promotion, but not if it meant relocation. Ask yourself: 'Where, when and with whom do I want/not want this outcome?'

5. Am I congruent about wanting this?

In NLP, being congruent means every part of you wants something. Ask yourself:

✓ 'What will it add to my life?'

✓ 'What will it allow me to do?'

✓ 'How much do I really want it?'

✓ 'Is it absolutely right for me?'

✓ 'Do I need to make adjustments to make me totally congruent about it?'

Another way of asking the same question is to think about what it is important to have, do or be in your life (see 'What do I want?', pp.80-1).

6. Is it only for me? Can I take responsibility for achieving this outcome?

Is your outcome under your control? If you need to involve other people, how can you take responsibility for persuading them to help you? How much can you do by yourself?

7. What resources do I have now and what resources will I need to get my outcome?

✓ Where are you right now? What are your resources in terms of:
Mental and emotional skills: intelligence and knowledge
Physical possessions: what you own, the money you have
People: your family and friends and the network of people you can ask for help
Models: the people you don't know but can study and learn from.

✓ What resources can you acquire or set up?
✓ What can you do straight away?
✓ Have you ever had or done this before? If not, do you know anyone who has? What would happen if you acted as if you had done it?
✓ What can you continue doing that you are already doing?

8. Is it good for me and my life?

The different parts of your life cannot be compartmentalized – they are part of a whole. Every outcome is likely to have a knock-on effect in other areas of your life, and on the environment, other people and the wider world.
Ask yourself:

✓ 'What will happen if I get this outcome? Are there secondary consequences I haven't considered?'

✓ 'What changes will occur in the rest of my life? Will I need to make adjustments by setting set outcomes in other areas?'

✓ 'What will I gain or lose if I get this outcome? Am I congruent about any sacrifices I may have to make?'

✓ 'How will it affect my family, friends and community?'

9. What is the first step?

When you have run an outcome through these questions, ask yourself: 'What is the first step I can take to achieve my outcome?' You may have the most congruent outcome and still do nothing to get it. Decide on some steps you can take towards getting it and the ones you can do immediately. How big is your outcome? Can it be broken down into several outcomes? Would that make it easier to think of steps towards it?

If you are not sure how to come up with a first step:

✓ Imagine you already have your outcome. Go to that place where you have achieved it.

✓ Now look back at now and all the time between now and the goal you have just achieved.

✓ What were the steps you took to reach your goal? Once an outcome has been experienced as if it has already happened, the brain becomes very creative. You will find you unconsciously begin to come up with lots of ways in which to attain it.

Write down the steps you can think of. It may help if you share your outcomes with someone you know. This may help you to commit to action, find support and resources, and sometimes gain extra clarity.

5-minute exercise: mental rehearsal
The technique known as 'mental rehearsal' fixes an outcome as a real experience in your future. Your brain processes it as if it is already real.
1. Think about an outcome you have clarified.
2. Imagine that you are already achieving that outcome. For example, if you want to ski down a red run, see yourself already doing it through your own eyes. Feel and hear the snow beneath your skis.
3. If any negative inner voices pipe up with reasons why this won't work, notice the purpose of this self-talk.
4. Can you change this self-talk? Are there any limiting beliefs or emotions to deal with?
5. Repeat making the pictures. Practice makes perfect.

EXAMPLE:

Here is an example of a goal that has been put through the outcome question process: I have increased my sales by 20% on the final day of July. The evidence is that I am looking at the figures in front of me and saying, 'Well done.' I am in my office. The consequences are that I can ask my employer for more money because of my improved performance. This is a goal that is achievable by me. I have resources: the support of my office and the know-how. I do need extra contacts. My first step is to plan how to build my client network.

THE DISNEY METHOD

The Disney method entails creative thinking around an outcome. It was modelled from Walt Disney and devised by Robert Dilts. Disney was enormously successful in coming up with big visions that came to fruition because he had the flexibility to have several points of view – those of the dreamer, the realist and the critic.

✓ The dreamer creates a vision for the future. He can define what he wants and the benefits of having it.

✓ The realist gives it a time frame and assesses who can carry it out.

✓ The critic assesses what is feasible and not feasible, and acts as a filter.

Many people are naturally able to take one of these positions when they evaluate their goals, but if you want to be successful in a creative endeavour, you need a little bit of all three.

Extended exercise: using the Disney method
Use this method when you need to come up with a creative goal or vision. Do it in order and give sufficient time to each step.

1. **The dreamer.** Brainstorm all the possibilities without introducing critique or realism. Ask yourself: 'What do I want?' 'Why?' 'What are the benefits?' 'What is the vision that will allow me to know when I have this?' 'Where do I want this idea to take me?' 'Who do I want to be in relation to manifesting this idea?'

2. **The realist.** Turn the vision into a plan. Ask yourself: 'When will the goal be completed?' 'Who is going to be involved?' 'How will I make sure it happens?' Define the first and subsequent steps. 'How will I know whether I am on or off course?' 'What evidence will indicate I have attained the goal?'

3. **The critic.** Check the consequences of realizing the vision. Ask yourself: 'When and where would I not want to implement this plan or idea?' 'What is currently missing from the plan?' 'Who will it affect?' 'Who could prevent or ensure the effectiveness of the idea?' 'What do I need to know about these people and what they need? What benefits are there for them?' 'Why might someone find fault with my plan?' 'What benefits are there in how I am doing things now? What have I got now? What am I now?' 'How can I keep those things when I have my goal?'

YOUR LANGUAGE

If you want to change the results in your life, you need to change the language you use. This is the *linguistic* part of Neuro-Linguistic Programming. The Meta Model (see p. 92) is an NLP tool you can use to examine what is underlying your choice of words. The Milton Model (see p. 100) is a tool for producing deep behaviour change unconsciously.

The language we use inside our heads (self-talk) and to others reveals our internal pictures or representations and thus our hidden thinking. Discovering your unconscious thought processes is the first stage in changing behaviour. Then you can reprogramme your behaviour using changes in language and thinking as well as other techniques.

From time to time you may find yourself unclear about another person's meaning. This may be because he has some gap in his thinking as a result of the way he distorts the world. You need to stop and ask a question to clarify what is going on.

When you are talking to somebody, always ask yourself what question will:
✓ get to the heart of the issue
✓ give the person new choices

✓ be the difference that makes a difference
✓ help them to get to their outcome.

Questioning can be used to:
✓ recover information
✓ get into a state
✓ set an outcome
✓ clarify or set a strategy.

It allows you to get under the surface structure of what is being said to discover what is going on at a deeper level – how you delete, distort and generalize your experience.

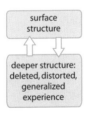

Why? Is the question least used in NLP because it is about reasons rather than about structure, strategy and process. It encourages blame rather than change.

What? Asks you to be specific in the information you give to the questioner. For example, 'What do you want as an outcome?' 'For what purpose?'

Who? Asks you to be specific about the people involved. For example, 'Who do you want that outcome with?' 'Who is usually present when you behave like that?'

How? Asks you for a process by which you do something – which can then be reprogrammed using NLP techniques. 'How do you behave specifically?'

Where? Asks you for a context or a location. 'Where do you want this outcome?'

When? Asks you to be specific about a time. 'When do you want this?'

THE META MODEL

John Grinder and Richard Bandler observed the questions that the therapists they modelled for NLP used to get below the surface issues their clients presented. As a result, they developed a specific set of questions that is known as the 'Meta Model'.

Meta Model questions get to the deeper levels of language and reveal what parts of someone's experience he has deleted, generalized or distorted out of his conscious awareness. Once you know this, you can discover what is behind his behaviour.

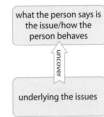

what the person says is the issue/how the person behaves

uncover

underlying the issues

Deletion, generalization and distortion are revealed in different ways in the language we use and there are different Meta Model questions for each, as follows.

Meta Model – Deletion

1. Nominalizations

Nominalizations are verbs that have been made into nouns. The rule is, if it's a noun and you can't put it in a wheelbarrow, then it's a nominalization.
Examples are:
'We had an understanding.'
'She values her independence.'
Meta Model responses:
'What specifically do you understand?'
'What about being independent is important to her?'

2. Unspecified verbs

Unspecified verbs are verbs where some detail of the action is not specified.

Examples are:
'He rejected me.'
'He touched me.'
Meta Model responses:
'How specifically did he reject you?'
'How did he touch you?'

3. Lack of referential index

Here an action is specified, but not the doer.

Examples are:
'They stole candy from my house.'
'It's not fair.'

Meta Model responses:
'Who stole candy from your house?'
'For whom is it not fair?'

4. Comparative deletions

Here a comparison is made, but what it is being compared to is unspecified. Comparative deletions include words like 'better', 'worse', 'more', 'less', 'best', 'worst'.

Examples are:
'I'm a better person.'
'She's the worst.'

Meta Model responses:
'Better than whom?'
'Compared to whom?'

Meta Model – Generalization

1. Universal quantifiers

These are words like 'always', 'all', 'every', 'everyone', 'never', 'no one'. By using these generalizations you limit your choices.

Examples are:

'He's always kinder to you than to me.'

'She never listens to what I am saying.'

'Everyone thinks I'm great!'

Meta Model responses:

'He's *always* kinder to you?'

'Never? Has there ever been a time when she listened to you?'

'Everyone?'

2. Modal operators

A modal operator is a word that implies possibility or necessity. There are three types of modal operators:

Possibility – can, will

Impossibility – can't, won't

Necessity – must, have to, it is necessary

Examples are:

'I can't do this.'

'I have to make the appointment.'

Meta Model responses:

'Have you ever been able to do this?'

'What would happen if you didn't go?'

By using these generalizations, you are limiting your choices.

Meta model – Distortion

1. Mind-reading

This is when you make an assumption about what another person means, feels or thinks. You impose your distortions onto him rather than recognizing that he may have different views, values and motives. This can lead to inaccurate and often negative thoughts and can therefore be harmful to relationships.

Examples are:

'He doesn't like me.'

'He loves me.'

Meta Model responses:

Inquire what the other person is thinking, and ask for some more evidence:

'How do you know he doesn't like you?'

'How do you know he loves you?'

2. Reversed/projected mind-reading

Mind-reading can work in another way as well. This is where you assume that the other person will, or should, know what you are thinking. You project onto him your expectations about what he should be able to understand.

Examples are:

'He should know what I like.'

'I know what's good for my own son.'

Meta Model responses:

Answer by challenging the evidence: 'How should he know what you like?'

'What leads you to believe that you know what's good for your son?'

3. Lost performative

A lost performative is a value judgement where the evidence on which the judgement was based has been left out of what is said. Lost performatives are expressed in the form of generalized standards or rules about the world. Who has set these standards is not mentioned.

Examples are:

'It's bad to be late.'

'That is a stupid idea.'

Meta Model responses:

'Who says it's bad to be late? According to whom is it bad to be late?'

'How do you know it's stupid? According to whom?'

To avoid making lost performative statements, be precise in your judgement and own what you say. Make 'I' statements.

For example:

'I believe that…'

'My opinion is…'

4. Cause and effect

A cause and effect statement implies that A causes B – that one person's action, communication or behaviour can directly cause a response in another person. It therefore implies there is a lack of choice.

This kind of thinking can cause a lot of pain within relationships.

If you feel that you have no choice but to respond in a certain way every time you encounter certain behaviour or attitudes, you are putting severe limitations on your own life.

In effect, you relinquish all responsibility for controlling your own emotional state, because you 'have' to have that reaction.

Examples are:

'If he leaves me, I will get depressed.'

'When he shouts at me, I will get angry.'

Meta Model responses:

Ask for a counter-example – an exception – that disproves the general rule that has been invented.

'How would him leaving you cause you not to get depressed?'

'Has he ever shouted at you and you not got angry?'

5. Complex equivalence

This is a statement that implies that A equals B.

Examples are:

'His being late means he doesn't like me.'

'I know he's angry because he gave me that look.'

Meta Model responses:

'How does his being late mean he doesn't like you?'

'How does his giving you that look mean he's angry?'

6. Presuppositions

Presuppositions are statements that assume that something is true or will be true.

Examples are:

'I'm concerned that my new boss will be as unreasonable as the last one.'

(There are several presuppositions in this statement: that the person had a boss who is no longer his/her boss, and that the previous boss was unreasonable.)

Meta Model responses:

'How specifically was your previous boss unreasonable?'

THE MILTON MODEL

The Milton Model is a breakdown of the language that the hypnotherapist Milton Erickson used with his patients to get them to change their patterns of behaviour. The Model is a way of using language to talk to the unconscious mind of another person.

The Milton Model contains a series of phrases and patterns of language that are almost the opposite. They include generalizations, ambiguous statements and indirect language. These language patterns may be indirectly suggestive. They actually have the effect of drawing someone inside himself to use his creative imagination.

With the Milton Model, the person goes into an altered state in which the conscious mind is distracted, leaving the unconscious mind free to listen to the language of the therapist. His unconscious mind interprets the Milton Model language as an instruction to access new resources and produce new ways of doing things.

The instructions are kept deliberately vague so that he has to dig deep into his unconscious resources to produce change easily and effortlessly. The Milton Model uses symbols, metaphors, images and positively phrased language that appeal to the unconscious mind that can induce a trance state and unleash his unconscious resources and imaginative powers.

The Meta Model, on the other hand, is precise and specific. It encourages you to become clear about what you have deleted, generalized and distorted so that you can communicate more efficiently with other people.

If you need to take someone out of an over-real personal world – in a way that is similar to breaking a trance – use the Meta Model and ask specific questions.

DIFFERENCES BETWEEN THE META MODEL AND THE MILTON MODEL

Milton

✓ Is general and vague.

✓ Accesses resources at an unconscious level.

✓ Uses deletions, distortions and generalization to bring about trance.

✓ Uses suggestions to produce behavioural change.

✓ Produces a trans-derivational search. The listener comes up with his own meanings.

Meta

✓ Is precise and specific.
✓ Brings resources into conscious awareness.
✓ Challenges deletions, distortions and
  generalization to break a trance.
✓ Asks questions to uncover what's going on
  underneath the surface language to produce
  behavioural change.

TRANCE

The Milton Model provides a list of very effective
language patterns that have a semi-hypnotic effect –
they are heard by the unconscious mind in such a
way as to produce a trance. The idea of trance is much
misunderstood. In fact it is simply a relaxed state in
which it becomes easier to communicate with the
unconscious mind and to access its resources.

Hypnosis is a means by which you can get yourself
into that relaxed state. You can be directed into a
trance state by another person or do it yourself. There
are several types of trance.

Natural trance

Trance is a natural state of relaxation. You probably go
into a light trance every day. When in a trance you are

unaware of time or experience it more quickly or slowly than normal.

Negative trance
When you brood obsessively about something and your thoughts go round in circles, you have created a negative trance. Your imagination is dragging you deeper into your own negative thoughts and feelings. Certain triggers, known as 'anchors', may take you into this trance as a matter of habit (see pp. 127-37).

Hypnotic trance
A hypnotic trance is simply a deliberately induced positive trance. It is a pleasant state of relaxation.

Shock/injury trance
If you have an accident and go into shock, you may not be aware of what has happened at first – even if you are seriously injured. This is a form of trance.

Indicators of trance
Other indicators of trance you may observe are:
✓ relaxed muscles throughout the body
✓ minimal movement
✓ the voice sounds relaxed and deeper
✓ the mouth may drop

- ✓ the eye muscles relax and the eyes may be slightly unfocused
- ✓ the breathing deepens and becomes slower
- ✓ hallucination
- ✓ anaesthesia
- ✓ amnesia – a person forgets what they have experienced while in trance
- ✓ catalepsy – the body becomes so still it can stay in the same position a long time

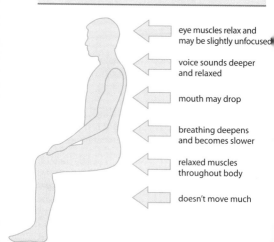

eye muscles relax and may be slightly unfocused

voice sounds deeper and relaxed

mouth may drop

breathing deepens and becomes slower

relaxed muscles throughout body

doesn't move much

Language and trance

Hypnotherapists use language – sometimes direct and authoritarian – to put a client into a trance. Some write scripts for helping their clients stop smoking or relieve stress.

Erickson was different. He didn't use scripts and his language was permissive and indirect, and included metaphors and stories. He adopted a variety of approaches depending on the needs and personalities of his clients, therefore bypassing any resistance that they might have had to therapy through flexible communication. He was particularly attuned to non-verbal communication and could observe the smallest changes in the patient's physiology. This alerted him to what effect his words were having.

MILTON MODEL LANGUAGE

The phrases on pp. 106-8 can be used to take someone into an altered state where he can access his inner resources and produce changes.

When you use these language patterns, observe the other person. Look for indicators of trance (see diagram left) to see the effect of your words.

Deletion

1. Comparative deletions

Here a comparison is made but it is not specified what it is in relation to. The other person is free to supply the information, e.g. 'It feels more or less the right time...'

2. Lack of referential index

This is a general phrase that could refer to anything in the person's experience, so he can imbue it with some meaning appropriate to him. For example: 'There are things around you that are important to you.'

3. Lost performative

This is a judgement where anything about who is making it, or why, is omitted. For example: 'It's great to remember the things you do well...'

Generalization

1. Universal quantifier

This is a phrase that contains a universal word, such as 'all', 'everyone', 'everything', inviting the listener to open up and go beyond his current thinking. For example: 'Everything you experience has value...'

2. Modal operator

A modal operator of possibility gives the listener permission, for example 'can', 'may'.

'You may find you meet people...'

A modal operator of necessity allows the listener to draw himself up new rules of behaviour, for example 'should', 'must'.

'You should take this opportunity to change...'

Distortion

1. Mind-reading

In mind-reading, you claim to know what is going on inside someone's head, for example: 'I know that you are understanding many new things about yourself as we talk...'

2. Complex equivalence

Here you state one thing as equal to the other, for example: 'The fact that you are relaxing means that you are making sense of things.' The suggestion is that relaxing is the equivalent of making sense, so the person relaxes more.

3. Nominalizations

Because nominalizations are vague, the unconscious has room to interpret them in a way that is appropriate for that person. For example: 'As your relaxation deepens, you find new insights and excitements.'

4. Cause and effect
This implies that one thing causes another to happen. For example: 'If you close your eyes, you will feel more relaxed.'

5. Presuppositions
This is an assumption that an outcome is going to happen. For example, 'I don't know how deep your trance is yet': by presupposing the person is in a trance you cause him to fall into one.

How to use the Milton Model
To use the Milton Model with another person, you need to help him go into a light trance and then to use your language in such a way that his unconscious mind will have permission to start looking for resources that take it towards the outcome that you have set up with him. Follow these stages.

1. First, pace the current experience of the person:
• Describe what the person is experiencing to him as he experiences it.
• Describe it in a way that is undeniable by him because what you are describing is what he is doing externally and involves no mind reading.
• This allows you and the other person to get into rapport and helps the person to go into trance. For example: 'You are sitting on the chair, listening

to my voice [pacing] and as you are hearing
it…you can begin to relax more [leading].'

2. Talk in ambiguous, general and vague language.
This allows you to talk to the person's unconscious
mind and get his conscious mind out of the way.
The ambiguity of the Milton Model language
distracts and confuses the conscious mind, aiding
the trance.

3. Introduce the deletion, generalization and
distortion language patterns of the Milton Model
to allow the other person to begin to access his
unconscious resources and start to change on an
unconscious level.

You don't need to know what is happening. All you
have to do while this is going on is to observe
(calibrate) the other person's physiology so that
you can see that pleasant changes are taking place.

4. Deepen the trance with additional language
patterns. As well as the language patterns given
above, there are several other ways of using the
language that Milton used. These will all increase
your effectiveness. We will look at these in more
depth on pages 110-113.

> **MILTON MODEL: AN EXAMPLE**
>
> 'I know that you are understanding new things…and
> it's really great that you are understanding new
> things… because…that means…you're already
> learning more at an unconscious level than you think
> you understand… and it's good to let the unconscious
> learn in any way it wants to. And since you are sitting on
> the chair, listening to my words, all the things you are
> hearing are allowing you to have new insights. And you
> have, haven't you…?'

ADDITIONAL MILTON PATTERNS

Grinder and Bandler modelled other language
patterns from Erickson that can deepen a trance.

Double binds
A double bind is when you appear to give
someone a choice, but in fact you predetermine
the extent of their choice, for example:'I don't
know whether you might like to do it now or in a
few minutes.'You have also presupposed that he
will actually do it.

Conversational postulates
This is a question that expects a 'yes' or a 'no'
answer. The person speaking uses permissive

language yet the listener's unconscious mind understands the question as an instruction, for example: 'Do you feel this…is something you can imagine?' 'Can you consider for a moment…?'

Tag questions

A tag question is 'tagged on' to a statement, for example: 'wouldn't you?', 'aren't they?' ('This is the quickest way to relax, isn't it?') It softens the statement and therefore displaces resistance. A series of tag questions is called a 'yes set'; after a 'yes set', the person is more likely to be open to what you say, as his unconscious mind is already convinced it agrees with you. Tag questions that mix past and present tenses can also be used to confuse the listener's conscious mind, for example: 'You can relax, didn't you?'

Embedded language

You can embed questions or commands by hiding them in a sentence so that they are only understood by the unconscious mind. Mark it by slightly changing the volume or speed of your speech, or by a brief pause after this part of the statement, much as if you have highlighted it. For example: 'I don't know whether you will go into trance right now.' (Command). 'I don't know whether you know what resources you need to change now?' (Question).

Extended quotes

Another way of sounding more permissive and less directive is to present a message in the form of a quotation, since you distance yourself from what is being said. For example: 'I went to America once and met a man who was very skilled at hypnosis, and he used to say that it was the easiest thing in the world to go into a trance!'

Restriction violation

The unconscious loves listening to stories. When you tell a story you can give inanimate objects or animals feelings or powers that a human would have. This is known as restriction violation. For example: 'A fly can have feelings...' 'The chair has a secret to share...'

Ambiguity

Ambiguity as a language pattern is used to distract and confuse the conscious mind so that the speaker can access the listener's unconscious mind more quickly. There are different types of ambiguity.

Phonological ambiguity

'Hear/here', 'buy now/by now', 'you're unconscious/your unconscious' are words and phrases that sound alike but have different meanings. This kind of ambiguity will make the listener do a trans-derivational search.

Syntactic ambiguity

This is where the syntactic function of a word is not clear from its context. Generally this works by adding '-ing' to make a noun a verb. For example: 'They are interesting people.' Are 'they' interesting 'the people' or are they themselves interesting?

Scope ambiguity

Here you use a phrase where the context does not make it clear whether it applies to all or just one portion of the sentence. For example: 'The fascinating sounds and sights…' Are the sights fascinating as well as the sounds? 'Speaking to you as a woman…' Am I a woman or are you?

Punctuation ambiguity

Here you let one sentence run into another to confuse conscious mind. For example: 'I want you to notice your hand me the pen.'

CHANGING YOUR PERSPECTIVE

You can bring about profound changes in your life simply by altering your perceptions of a past or present situation. NLP has several techniques that you can use to do this. They will provide you with more choice in your life and can enhance your relationship with other people.

One of the central beliefs of NLP is that you hold all the resources you need inside you. Use these resources to change your states of mind and increase your motivation.

CHUNKING

Chunking is an easy technique you can use to create new choices. When we deal with information, we break it up, or 'chunk' it, to make it easier to deal with. Sometimes we use large or 'big picture' chunks. Sometimes we use small or 'detail' chunks.

People can habitually think at a big picture, general, large chunk level, or at a detailed, specific, small chunk level. Miscommunication can arise if one person is focusing at a different level from another. To create communication, you can 'chunk up' or 'down' or 'sideways' to meet the other person at a level that he can understand. This is a very effective technique

to use when you want to achieve a win-win scenario.
When you chunk differently it gives you a new
perspective on an issue.

How to chunk up, down and sideways

• To move from the specific to the general, chunk
up – ask, 'What is this an example of?'
• To move from the general to the specific, chunk
down – ask, 'What is an example of this?'
• To move sideways – ask, 'What is another example
of this?'
• To chunk up on a habit or behaviour – ask 'What is
the positive intention behind this behaviour?'
• To chunk up on your outcomes – ask, 'If I have this
outcome, what will that give me?'

To negotiate, chunk up until you find agreement:
Person A says, 'I want to eat pizza.'
Person B says, 'I want to eat pasta.'
What are both these foods examples of? Italian food.
They can agree to go to an Italian restaurant.

The Meta Model chunks from general to specific. The
Milton Model chunks from specific to general.
The model of chunking is known as the 'Hierarchy of
Ideas'. For example, in the picture on page 116,
mammals are a specific example of an animal.

From big picture to detail

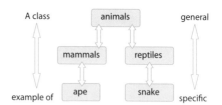

Chunking sideways

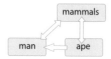

PERCEPTUAL POSITIONS

We naturally take different positions at different times. Sometimes we see things very strongly only from our own vantage point. At other times, we step into other people's shoes and look at the world from that perspective. Sometimes we may stand back from a situation totally so that we can look dispassionately at what is happening. These different viewpoints are called 'perceptual positions' in NLP.

They were developed by John Grinder and Judith DeLozier, drawing on work originally done by Gregory Bateson. The technique allows you to gain multiple perspectives on a particular interaction.

It is important to realize that there is no such thing as one 'correct' perspective. Each person has only a partial understanding and sees things through his own blinkers. You don't have to agree with the other person, but if you can see things from his perspective it stops you being rigid in your thinking and opens up greater levels of understanding.

You can use the perceptual positions technique either to look at a situation after it has happened (review), or before it has happened (mental rehearsal/preview). It is particularly useful where there is a block in understanding between the people involved or where you feel stuck in a particular way of thinking about a situation.

It can be used in business negotiations. Any resolution of a relationship conflict or a negotiation involves the perspectives of all the people involved, and coming up with a solution that allows everyone to feel satisfied – in other words, it is a 'win-win' scenario.

5-minute exercise: using the perceptual positions technique

Choose a situation in which there is conflict between you and another person. In your mind, put yourself into each of three positions in turn.

1. In position one, see the situation as it is happening to you. Notice your opinions and your values. What does it look like, sound like and feel like to you? What do you feel and think? What are your beliefs and outcomes?

2. In position two, put yourself in the other person's shoes. How is that person thinking about the same

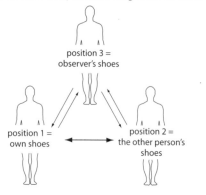

position 3 =
observer's shoes

position 1 =
own shoes

position 2 =
the other person's
shoes

situation? Imagine what he feels to be true. What does it look like, sound like and feel like? What are his beliefs and outcomes?

3. In the third position, what do you observe about the relationship between the people in positions one and two? What new perspective do you get here? What do the two positions have in common? How are they related? Pay attention to their communication and their non-verbal behaviour. What are the common elements in their outcomes? What advice can you give them from your objective position?

4. Now repeat the process again.

5. At the end of the round, step back into your own shoes in position one. Notice what you have learned about yourself, the other person and the whole situation. What new choices do you have available to you now?

THE META MIRROR

The Meta Mirror is a further technique, developed by Robert Dilts, that draws on the ideas of perceptual positions. In this technique, you use different positions to look at another person's viewpoint. It adds a fourth position to the three in the previous technique.

You can either do the Meta Mirror technique inside your head or actually move around to each position in turn. In this technique, the idea is that how another person treats you is a reflection of the way you see and behave towards yourself.

You can use this technique to review or preview a meeting where you will be talking to another person about an issue you don't entirely agree on, or after an interaction in which you didn't come to a positive conclusion for both of you.

If you have something to say to another person and you don't know what their reaction will be, do this technique and imagine how that person will respond to what you have to say to him.

The Meta Mirror is a 'content-free' technique. You do not need to discuss the content of the situation you are recalling or previewing. It works best by you processing your thoughts inside yourself. It provides a safe context in which you can shift positions to deal with limitations, conflicts and issues inside the dynamic of the relationship to produce an outcome that is positive for all the parties involved.

5-minute exercise: using the Meta Mirror technique

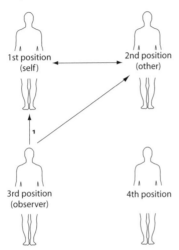

1st position (self)

2nd position (other)

3rd position (observer)

4th position

Decide what interaction/relationship you would like to use the technique for; for example, an unsatisfactory conversation you had with another person. (If this is the first time you have used the technique, choose a relationship where it will be helpful to improve communication but not the worst you have.)

1. In position one (self), look at the other person and ask yourself, 'What do I see, hear, feel and think in this position about the relationship/interaction?'

2. Then step into the other person's shoes, position two. Imagine how the situation looks from that person's point of view. If it helps, get into his way of sitting or standing.

3. Now, go to position three. Be an observer, detached from the situation. Notice the relationship between the two people (one and two). What do you notice about their relationship and their interaction?

4. Add another position (position four) from which you can observe the interaction between the two people as well as the observer. Notice the relationship between position one and position three and the insights position three has had about position one. Notice the same for positions two and three.

5. Finally, go back to each position in turn, thinking about any additional resources and insights you have when you take this perspective and would like to integrate for the future as a conscious resource. End by coming back to yourself in the now. Think of a time in the future when these resources and insights you have discovered in yourself may be useful. Notice how you will know that it is time to access these new resources you have just gained from this exercise.

REFRAMING

Have you ever changed the frame on a picture? Did it suit the smaller or the bigger frame?

Imagine that it is raining on a summer's day. Is that good or bad? That depends whether you are a farmer needing water for your crops or whether you have chosen today for your garden party. A central belief of NLP is that all meaning is context-dependent. If you change the context, you can change the meaning. Negative emotions about a situation are not caused by the situation itself but by how you view it. By looking at things from a different perspective, you can create positive emotions and new choices.

You can reframe a situation. This way, you can choose what reaction you will have to a situation.

How to change your view

If you change the

✓ situation
✓ time frame
✓ context

your perceptions of the same situation will change, because all meaning is dependent upon the context in which it is set. Jokes, fairy tales and children's stories are full of reframes. In some fairy tales, a situation might arise that the reader views as terrible; however, by the end of the story you realize that all was not as it seemed. For example, in *The Ugly Duckling*, the ugly duckling turns out to be a beautiful swan.

EXAMPLE:

What if you were to lose your job? In the short term, it might seem like a disaster for many reasons. But if you look at it in a longer time frame, you might realize that it gives you the chance to step back and reassess what it is you want out of life. Perhaps you could go on to start a new career in a different area entirely.

The words we select can be used as frames to point to the meaning we want others to hear:

- 'Unfortunately…he lost his job.'
- 'Amazingly…he lost his job.'
- 'The price is £1,999. That's *under* £2,000.'
- 'The price is £1,999. That's *nearly* £2,000.'

Context reframes and meaning reframes

You can break reframes down into two types: context and meaning. Both reframes ask you to look at how a behaviour could have a different value or meaning if you look at it in a different way.

Context reframe

Here are a few phrases that signal you could use a context reframe: 'I'm too...' 'He's too...' 'I wish I could do this more...' When a person uses these words, he is complaining that he (or another person) acts in a particular way in a particular context. He has *generalized* the behaviour and deleted the fact that this behaviour takes place within a *specific* context.

5-minute exercise: context reframe

Think of a generalization you make, for example:

- 'He's too...detail-orientated for this job.'
- 'She's too easy-going to tell her staff off.'

You can reframe by pointing out that the same behaviour may be useful in a different context, for example:

- 'He would be a great proofreader – it needs a lot of attention to detail.'
- 'She's easy-going. She has lots of friends as a result.'

Meaning reframe

You can use a meaning (content) reframe when you would like your response to something to be more positive.

Ask yourself, 'What else could this mean? What is the positive value of this?' Or, if you are helping another person, ask yourself: 'What is it that he hasn't noticed (in this context) that will reveal a different meaning and change his response?'

For example: 'When I have to do public speaking, I start to feel anxious.' What is the positive value of this? Perhaps that you prepare more thoroughly. Perhaps the motivation and adrenaline improve your speech.

5-minute exercise: applying reframing to your life
1. Think of events in your own life that you would like to see in a more positive light, perhaps something you have classified as a 'mistake'.
2. Apply a context reframe or a meaning reframe.
3. Notice if you begin to highlight or focus on different aspects of the experience. What are the advantages of the situation that you can now make work for you? For example, you may have chosen to take a job with a firm, but you have ethical concerns about a product that the company produces so you resign. However, you did learn some skills while you were there, and you can bring these to a job that you find more rewarding.

ANCHORS

Anchors are a very simple way to tap into your unconscious resources. An anchor is an unconscious trigger that can be applied to produce a positive state of mind and to change your behaviour.

Anchors occur in everyday life. They are set up automatically by an intense emotion that has become linked to an experience. When you come into contact with the anchor at a later date it triggers off some of the original associations. If the emotion has been very intense it may set up a phobia. If it is less intense but the experience has occurred repeatedly, it may still set up an anchor.

Behavioural psychologists would point out that our behaviour is composed of anchors. There are many naturally occurring anchors in everyday life that change our mood from one moment to another.

States produced by naturally occurring anchors can be positive or negative. A particular way of speaking, facial expression and/or gesture can trigger off anger, or leave you feeling sad, and these feelings often occur to a greater extent than seems logical in the context because a past experience has anchored you to a negative emotion linked to these experiences.

Pavlov

The Soviet scientist Ivan Pavlov famously experimented on dogs to show how conditioning can trigger a response. When he sounded a tuning fork at the same time as feeding a dog a steak, the idea of the steak and the sound became linked together neurologically in the dog's brain. When he took the steak away and still sounded the tuning fork, the dog still salivated. Out of this comes the idea that you can apply a specific stimulus to any intense experience and link the two together.

Anchors and the senses

Random everyday anchors can occur in all five senses: visual, auditory, kinaesthetic, gustatory (taste) and olfactory (smell). Examples might include:

• If you smell a scent that you link with someone you were once in love with, you will feel some emotion because the smell has triggered an association with the past feeling.

• How a piece of satin feels might bring back the memory of a wedding dress.

• What you feel when you hear the sound of a police siren may depend on whether you are a criminal or victim.

• What about the sight of a school desk?

• The taste of a food you have only had on a sunny and happy holiday might bring back some of the happiness you felt then even if you are eating it on a cold and miserable day at work.

EVERYDAY TRIGGERS (ANCHORS)

Auditory
train whistle; motorcycle motor

Visual
a smile; a fist gesture

Olfactory/gustatory (smell/taste)
fresh bread; cigarette smoke

Kinaesthetic (touch and feel)
a hand on your back; freshly laundered sheets

Some anchors can occur in more than one representational system. For example, the taste, sight and feel of a cigarette might all be anchors.

Extended exercise: resource anchors

A resource anchor is an anchor you set to change your emotional state and introduce positive resources into a situation. Set them up in six steps:

1. Decide on a positive state

What state would be most positive for you in a particular context? Here are a few to consider: happy, joyful, confident, highly motivated, completely relaxed, loving, elated. What if you were nervous about a meeting? What would be a good emotion to be feeling as you walk through the door? Choose a strong experience and a compelling state.

2. Elicit and calibrate the state

Think of the state you want to anchor. Elicit it by recalling a time when you felt that way naturally. Make sure you are associated into the past experience, as if you are there now. (A dissociated memory won't evoke the same emotion.) If this is difficult, shift your body around.

Instruct yourself: 'Think of a time when you felt this positive state. Go back to this time. See what you saw. Feel what you felt. Hear what you heard.' Once you are experiencing the feeling as if it is happening to you now, apply an anchor (stimulus) at its peak. Next time you want to recall the feeling, just reapply the anchor and you will feel the same way.

If you are working with another person, model the state you want him to get into – i.e., adjust your body and get into the state yourself. Then ask him questions to guide him into the state. If you have good rapport with the person, you can lead him there (see pp. 66-8).

You will need to calibrate him to make sure that he is feeling the appropriate amount of emotion. (Remember, 'to calibrate' means 'to observe what changes are happening in another person using your powers of observation'.)

3. Select an anchor
Choose an anchor – it can be a visual, auditory or kinaesthetic. A good kinaesthetic anchor would be to touch your knuckle because it is not a place that people normally touch. Another would be your heart.

4. Anchor the state
As the feeling approaches its peak of intensity, anchor it by touching your knuckle with your finger. As soon as the experience peaks, let go (to avoid anchoring a second state). Hold your finger down for 5–15 seconds, no more.

If you want, you can anchor more than one state at a time. Break state (see p. 46) by thinking about something else for a few seconds. If you are anchoring someone else, ask him an unrelated question to take his mind out of the previous state. Anchor the next state in the same place in the same way.

Break state and then continue stacking several states in this manner. You can add to this anchor any time you are in a positive state so that it will become more powerful every time you use it.

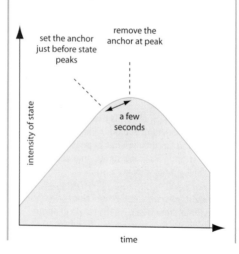

5. Test the anchor
See whether it works by touching the same place on your knuckle with your finger. If you have anchored the state(s) correctly you will observe a shift in yourself (or the other person). Is the feeling as compelling as you want it to be? If not, go back and stack more states (or the same state again).

6. Future pace
Think of a situation where in the past you might have felt negative. (Or take the other person through this process.) Imagine firing off the anchor. How positive do you feel at this point in the future?

Collapse anchors
To get rid of negative states it is useful to collapse old anchors. If you anchor two states then trigger them at the same time, the weaker one collapses into the stronger one.

To get rid of a negative feeling you stack a series of strong, compelling positive states in the same way that you would for a resource anchor and collapse a negative state into it. The next time you try to access the negative state it will bring up the positive state because the two are linked neurologically. This leaves a feeling of a neutral emotion.

Extended exercise: collapsing anchors

1. Choose the negative or unresourceful state you are going to collapse.

2. Choose appropriate positive states to stack. You can either stack one state as a resource anchor several times or choose several different positive states.

3. Anchor the positive states you have chosen onto one of your/the person's knuckles in the same way as for a resource anchor. Repeat this several times. If you are working with another person, make sure he is associated into the states. Help him by getting into the states too.

4. Break state. If you are working with another person, ask him to do something to focus his attention elsewhere for a few minutes. This takes you out of the positive states.

5. Elicit and calibrate the negative state. Anchor the negative state once only on a different knuckle.

6. Fire the two anchors together by touching the knuckles at the same time. Watch as the states come up to peak and integration takes place.

7. If working with another person, calibrate to check that integration has taken place. You will notice changes in his skin colour, breathing and other physical changes within a few seconds.

8. As soon as integration has occurred, release your finger from the negative anchor first while

continuing to hold down the positive anchor for a
further 5 seconds.
9. Break state. When you are working with
someone else, ask him to do something to focus
his attention elsewhere for a few minutes.
10. Test the anchor. Fire the negative anchor by
touching your knuckle or asking the other person
to touch his knuckle. If it works, you will feel/notice
a neutral rather than a negative state.

Chaining anchors

Naturally occurring states can work in chains. One
anchor triggers off a state, then that triggers off
another state, potentially spiralling into a more
negative feeling over a period of time.

You can design a chain of anchors to replace this and
to take you from an unresourceful state to a more
positive state.

Extended exercise: chaining anchors
1. Identify the state you no longer want to feel. If
you are working with another person, make sure
you have named it in specific terms using that
person's language.
2. Choose the positive and resourceful state you
would like to feel instead. Again, if you are working

with another person, make sure you have named it in specific terms using his language.

3. What states would best take you from the beginning state to the end state? Choose at least one link state.

4. Elicit and calibrate the first state. Anchor it to knuckle number one.

5. Break state and test it to make sure it is anchored correctly.

6. Anchor the next states to different knuckles. Break state between each one and test them.

7. Fire anchor one. As you reach the peak of the state, hold down anchor one and fire anchor two. If you are working with another person, ask him to signal you when he is reaching the peak of the state, then hold down anchor one and fire anchor two.

8. Release anchor one and hold anchor two. As anchor two reaches the peak of the state, fire anchor three while holding anchor two.

9. Repeat this process until you reach the final anchor. Let go of the final anchor. Break state.

10. Repeat the whole chain in the same way three times.

11. Fire anchor one. It should move you/the person through the whole chain of states so that you/he go into the end state automatically.

12. Future pace the chain. Imagine (or ask the person to imagine) a time in the future where in the past you (he) would have felt the old unresourceful state. Do you go into the positive state instead? Calibrate to check that the person goes into a positive state.

REMOVING BLOCKS

This chapter outlines a number of techniques you can use to overcome internal resistance or blocks set up by habitual ways of thinking or by rules you have devised for yourself, opening up avenues for action, behavioural change and fresh outcomes.

ALIGNED AND CONGRUENT CHANGE

If you are not congruent about making a change, as you start to take action your unconscious may throw up doubts or reasons why you can't progress – taking action is one of the best means of revealing deeply held belief, emotion and value blocks.

Chunking

We already know how chunking can shed light on a situation (see pp. 114-16). When faced with a block, you can use chunking to become more congruent about getting your outcome.

If you are having problems changing behaviour, ask yourself: 'What does this do for me?', 'What is the purpose of this?' If you are having problems moving towards an outcome, ask yourself: 'What will this do for me?' Then ask: 'What prevents me from achieving my outcome?' With behaviour, ask yourself, 'What other way of behaving would satisfy the same outcome?'

THE LOGICAL LEVELS MODEL

The way to create permanent change is to make sure that any change is congruent by making changes that are aligned at all levels of your being. A useful model to refer to is The Logical Levels or Neurological Levels model. It was developed by Robert Dilts and inspired by the work of Gregory Bateson.

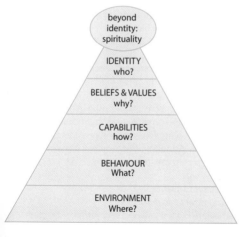

According to this model, change can take place at any of six different levels of the mind. The more abstract (or higher) levels dominate the less abstract (lower) levels. A change at a lower level may have a slight influence or no influence on a higher level. But a change at a higher level inevitably influences the lower levels. The biggest changes will come when you make changes at an identity level – the deepest level. You can use this model to create aligned outcomes: check what environment you want, how you want to act, what skills you want, what beliefs will be needed and what identity you want. Listen to your language to become aware of blocks at any level. (See examples below in *italics*.)

1. Environment: where and when
'I find I can't achieve anything in this environment. It all goes wrong when I am here.'
Where and when, context, or 'being in the right place at the right time' can influence your results. You may find opportunities for success in one context and constraints in another. What context, place or situations help you achieve success?

2. Behaviour: what
'I don't want to do that.'
Behaviour is what you do. Every action or reaction

results in an outcome. The outcome may be one you have chosen, or something you are entirely unconscious of. A block here may mean you need information about what to do instead.

3. Capability/skills: how

'I wish I found it easy to take action/do more things. I can't do it.'

Some of your skills – how you do things – as well as the strategies you follow in your day-to-day life are unconscious habits. Others were consciously acquired – for example, learning to drive. If you have a block at this level you may know what to do but doubt your ability to do it.

4. Beliefs and values: why

'That's not important to me.' 'I can't do things like that.'

Beliefs and values direct us in what we think is important to us and why. They act as permissions and as motivations. If you believe it is important to work hard, you will be motivated to go out and do so. If you believe you are too ugly to ever have a relationship, you may not find it easy to believe an admirer is really interested in you. 'Can't' is an indicator of a belief. What is important to you indicates a value. Use the belief and value change processes to combat blocks.

5. Identity: who
'I am a bad person.'
Identity is who you believe you are – your sense of
self. It is made up of your core beliefs and values as
well as your purpose in life. 'I am' or 'I am not' are
identity-level statements. Because an identity is
supported very strongly by many different beliefs,
you may have to undo a cluster of limiting beliefs and
values to create change at this level.

6. Spirituality: purpose
'I have lost any sense of a higher purpose.'
An individual or group may have a sense of
connection with something at a higher level for you –
a greater purpose or a spiritual meaning. To create a
vision at this level, ask yourself, 'What can I contribute
to the world?' or 'What am I here for?'

A change at this level can have a profound influence
on all other levels. This is why someone who has a
spiritual conversion may make an immense life
change. Check that changes you make at other levels
are aligned with your sense of higher purpose.

How the Logical Levels Model works
Successful outcomes and individuals are aligned
throughout all six levels. Here is an example:

✓ Spirituality: 'My purpose is to bring good to the world.'
✓ Identity: 'I am a good person.'
✓ Beliefs and values: 'Social work helps needy people and is a good thing.'
✓ Capability: 'I have the skills to help the people who are needy.'
✓ Behaviour: 'Every day I meet people and help them.'
✓ Environment: 'The place where I live and work has lots of people who need help.'

CHANGING BELIEFS THAT LIMIT YOU

Do you have any beliefs about yourself or the world that stop you achieving your outcomes or make you feel negative about yourself? What do you really believe (distinct from what you feel you 'should' believe)? As soon as you identify the beliefs you don't want, you can change them.

5-minute exercise: changing limiting beliefs
Do a simple brainstorm with yourself.
1. Take an area of your life and ask yourself: 'What do I believe/not believe about this?' List anything that comes into your mind, however illogical or irrational it may seem. Go on writing until you run out of anything to write.

2. Examine what you have written.
- Are these useful beliefs to hold?
- Do any of these beliefs limit you, either generally or in a specific context?
- What belief might be more useful?

MODELLING SUCCESSFUL BELIEFS

You may be able to think of a successful person you could model to acquire some new beliefs:

✓ Who do you know personally who has useful and positive beliefs in the area in which you want to change your beliefs?

✓ In what way do his beliefs differ from yours?

✓ What does he believe about himself?

✓ What does he believe about the world?

✓ What does he believe about the subject you are thinking about?

SUBMODALITIES

Submodalities are the fine distinctions by which we all make our own experience of the world, and store or code our experience inside our brains. These are principally related to the senses – visual, auditory and kinaesthetic, but can be olfactory and gustatory.

5-minute exercise: submodalities

Learn to identify your submodalities.

1. Think for a moment of a time when you felt really happy. Do you have a picture? Observe the visual distinctions within the picture. These are the visual submodalities. Ask yourself about the picture.

- ✓ Is it bright/dim?
- ✓ Focused/unfocused?
- ✓ Colour/black-and-white?
- ✓ Framed/panoramic?
- ✓ Are you dissociated, seeing yourself in the picture?
- ✓ Are you associated into it, seeing it through your own eyes?

2. Do you have any feelings in your body when you think of this time?

- ✓ Where can you feel this?
- ✓ Is there temperature/weight/texture?

3. What about any auditory elements? What can you hear?

- ✓ Is it loud/soft, fast/slow?
- ✓ Is there a rhythm?

4. Now think of a time when you were feeling a different emotion. What is your picture this time? How about any auditory or kinaesthetic elements?

5. As you do this, notice that every state and emotion is encoded differently within our brains. There may be two or three key submodality differences between the happy memory and your other memory.

How to change beliefs using submodalities

We hold our beliefs inside our brains in the same way as our emotions, using pictures or auditory and kinaesthetic submodalities.

You can change your beliefs by simply changing the picture you store. By changing the encoding of the belief – the submodalities – to those of a different belief, the first belief will be replaced by the second belief.

5-minute exercise: belief change

You can use the submodalities technique for getting rid of limiting and disempowering beliefs.
1. Identify a belief you hold to be true.
2. Identify a belief you don't hold to be true (non-belief).
3. Check the submodalities of each one. What are the pictures, sounds and feelings that make it up? (You should only pay attention to the *features* that structure the picture, not the *content* of the picture.)

4. To discover the *critical* submodalities ('drivers'), compare the two lists you have for each belief. What are the key differences?

5. If you switch the submodalities of the picture you have for your belief into the one you have for your non-belief, you will find that you no longer hold the original belief.

Extended exercise: installing a new belief

You can use submodalities to replace an old belief that no longer helps you with a positive one. This technique can be used for yourself or for another person.

Part one

1. Think of a belief about yourself that you wish you did not have (Belief A).

2. What are the submodalities – the pictures, sounds and feelings that make it up? Only pay attention to the features that structure the picture, not its content.

3. Next, think of a belief you had that is no longer true (Belief B).

4. What are the submodalities – the images, sounds and feelings that make up the picture in your mind?

5. Now compare the list of submodalities you have for beliefs A and B. You will find that there are some key differences. For example, one may be in black-and-white and one in colour. Maybe only one has auditory or kinaesthetic submodalities. These differences reveal the ways in which your brain stores different types of belief.

6. Retrieve the picture for Belief A. Now change the picture you have into the submodalities of Belief B. For example, if Belief A was associated, and Belief B was dissociated, make the picture dissociated.

7. Test your original belief. By coding it in a different way in your brain, you should find that you no longer believe it.

Part two

1. Now think of a belief that is absolutely true – that you live on this planet, for example (Belief C).

2. Do you have a picture? Check its submodalities – all the visual, auditory and kinaesthetic qualities – but again, ignore the content. It doesn't matter if you only have one type of submodality.

3. Think of a belief that you don't yet have but wish to have (Belief D). This is probably the opposite of belief A that limited you. What are its submodalities?

4. Now compare the list of submodalities you have for beliefs C and D. You will find again that there

are some key differences because of the way your brain codes your different beliefs.

5. Change the submodalities of the belief that you want to be true into the submodalities of the belief that is absolutely true.

6. Now test your new beliefs. What do you believe? You will find that you have a new belief that is absolutely true for you.

SWISH PATTERNS

A visual swish pattern is a technique that is used to change behaviour through changing the way you code that behaviour in your brain. The technique works as follows:

Extended exercise: swish patterns

1. First identify the behaviour or habit you want to change (present state). It may be something you do, for example eat too much chocolate, or something you don't do, for example act confidently in a certain situation.

2. Get a picture of the behaviour. How do you know when to do it? What is the visual trigger for it? Is it a picture inside your head? Or something you see in the real world?

3. Make the picture associated.

4. Identify the critical submodalities that make the picture what it is. Size, location and brightness are often critical submodalities. Now play with them to see if you can make the picture more or less compelling. Try making it bigger, smaller, brighter, duller, nearer, further away. If your feelings about it change, then these are the critical submodalities.

5. Break state. Do something to take your mind off the picture for a moment.

6. Now imagine the behaviour or habit you do want (desired state). Make this picture compelling so that you really feel motivated to have this in your life.

7. Check the picture is good for you and your life as a whole.

8. Make it dissociated.

9. Break state.

10. Now go back to the original picture, your unwanted behaviour, and ramp up the critical submodalities. For example, if size is important, make it very large. If brightness is important, make it very bright. There should be two main submodalities that make the difference. Make sure you are still associated.

11. Take your second picture, the desired state, and shrink it down into a small, dissociated picture into the bottom left-hand corner of your vision.

12. Swish. As quickly as you can, switch the two pictures. The unwanted behaviour shrinks down into the bottom left-hand corner, becoming a dark dot. The new desired behaviour swishes across becoming big and bright (or gains your two critical submodalities). Make a swish sound as you do it.

13. Blank your mind. Break state and look somewhere else for a few seconds.

14. Now repeat the swish.

15. Break state and repeat the swish several times – at least three.

16. Test. You will find that the picture of your old behaviour probably won't be the same any more.

17. Future pace. How are you going to behave in the future? See what picture comes into your head.

PHOBIAS

A phobia is set up when someone has had an unpleasant experience and has anchored the strong negative emotion to something – for example, an aeroplane, snake or spider. Next time he comes into contact with that thing, it will trigger the same response. However, it is possible to decode the experience using NLP techniques and teach the brain to replace the phobic response with new and positive emotions.

Extended exercise: curing phobias

Do this with another person so that you can guide him when he needs to be disassociated.

1. Ask him to recall his phobia. Ensure he only thinks about it very briefly and avoids associating into the emotion. Calibrate any changes in his physiology so that you can make comparisons with his response afterwards.

2. Break his state so he can get out of this physiology.

3. Establish a resource anchor (see pp. 129-33). Once this is done, he can always get back a positive emotion by triggering this anchor.

4. Now ask him to imagine he is in the projection room of a cinema watching a film below and in front of him.

5. Ask him to ask his unconscious mind to project the first intense experience that led to the phobia. (He will come up with something even if he is not certain that it is the first.)

6. Keep him dissociated from it by having him watch a film of himself from just before it happened (when everything was pleasant) to the point afterwards (when everything felt safe again). He should make the film black-and-white, since colour can intensify emotion.

7. Freeze the final frame of the film and white (or black) it out.

8. Break state.

9. Now ask him to associate into the end of the film (where it feels safe). Run the whole film back as quickly as possible in colour to the beginning, staying associated.

10. Break state.

11. Repeat this at least three times until he can no longer feel the original emotions. (If you are using this technique for a memory rather than a phobia, repeat it until the memory can't be accessed.)

12. Check the ecology. Is it OK for him to have changed this reaction? Will he need to behave differently in the future? Does he need additional resources? You can do a swish pattern at this point (see p. 149). Ensure he has appropriate responses to his previous phobia (for example, is he still cautious about a dangerous animal?)

13. Test and future pace.

TURNING A PROBLEM INTO AN OPPORTUNITY

How do you bring about change? How do you do anything you have never done before? By experimentation and making lots of mistakes. Successful people use their mistakes in a creative way. They take everything that happens to them as a process of feedback. Here's how to turn a problem into an opportunity.

- ✓ **Elicit**. Clarify what the 'problem' is. State it in detailed terms.
- ✓ **Brainstorm**. List all the possible ways in which you can solve the problem. You should count in any options at this point. Let your unconscious generate as many possibilities as possible. Keep your conscious logical mind out of the picture at this stage.
- ✓ **Logic**. Now use your conscious, logical mind. For each possibility you have written down, write down the steps that you would need to take to achieve it.
- ✓ **Consequences**. Look at the consequences of each option. Ask yourself what would happen if you take those steps.
- ✓ **Ecology**. What effect would pursuing each option have on your life?
- ✓ **Values**. What values do you have for this part of your life? How does each option fulfil or conflict with your values in this area?
- ✓ **Future pace**. What will it feel like, sound like, look like when you take each option? Which option is most appealing to you?
- ✓ **Action**. What is the first step you are going to take to achieve your outcome?

CHANGING VALUES

A value is what motivates you, or what is important to you – the 'why'. You need to change your values when they are not in alignment with a specific outcome and/or your general purpose in life.

Extended exercise: discovering values

1. Pick an area of your life you want to change, for example your career, relationship or money. What are your values? What's important to you about…? Write down the answers.

2. Number your values according to their importance. Ask yourself: 'Which of the above values is the most important to me?' 'If I had value X and not value Y, would that be OK?' 'What if it were the other way around?'

3. Rewrite the list of values according to the importance.

4. What does value X/Y mean to you? Asking for the meaning or *complex equivalence* of a word can tweak our deeper values and unconscious beliefs. The meaning *you* give to a word, such as 'challenge' or 'happiness', is what's important – not how another person interprets it.

5. Identify whether your values are carrot or stick. If you are motivated by 'stick' rather than 'carrot', your motivation strategy may be uncomfortable at times.

6. Are your values aligned? Each value should support the one above it. If it doesn't, you can use the changing values process below.
• Did your motivation include words like 'should', 'ought', 'have to' or any 'away from' motivations? Check for any limiting beliefs.
• Do you want two things simultaneously?
To resolve conflicting values, use the parts integration technique (see next page).
7. These are key values. To elicit them, look at your values list for a particular area. Ask yourself: 'If I had all these values, what would make me leave the situation?' Your answer is your 'threshold value'. Add it to your list, then ask 'and if this value too is present what would make me stay?' If you get another answer, add this to your list.

5-minute exercise: changing values technique
To change the position of a value in a hierarchy you use a similar technique to a belief change.
1. Discover (elicit) the submodalities of the value you wish to replace (A).
2. Elicit the submodalities of the value you wish to replace it with (B).
3. Take picture B and change the submodalities to those of picture A.

4. Elicit the values hierarchy list again and check that B is where you want it to be.

PARTS INTEGRATION

Sometimes a block to your outcomes occurs because one part of you wants one thing and another part wants another seemingly incompatible outcome. For example, one part of you wants to lose weight but the other part wants to eat that piece of chocolate. One part of you wants to be rich and successful but the other part always seems to sabotage you just as you are about to make it big. One part of you wants to make people happy, the other part feels angry and resentful.

You might even hear yourself using the expression, 'a part of me', or similar words such as 'one side' or 'on the one hand and on the other hand'. This is an indication of incongruity and conflict within your unconscious.

Sometimes these parts may operate at the same time (making yourself simultaneously incongruent). At other times, you will focus on one outcome one day but find yourself wanting the opposite outcome the next day (sequential incongruence).

Each part will have a positive intention for you, but unless you address this conflict, the block will remain. The parts integration technique can be used to resolve this incongruity. For every part, there is an opposite part. When you integrate them together the original conflict disappears.

Extended exercise: parts integration technique

1. Identify the part of you which is producing unwanted behaviour or results. Give it a name.
2. Hold your hands out in front of you and ask the unwanted behaviour or state part to come out onto one hand. Then ask the second part which is in conflict with it (its polar opposite) to come out on your other hand. Give it a name.
3. Get a visual, kinaesthetic and auditory representation of each part.
4. One part at a time, uncover the positive intention of each part: what is the intention/ purpose (of the behaviour)?
5. For each answer, chunk up: ask 'if you had that, what would that get you?' Eventually, you will reach a common purpose or intention for each part.
6. Point out to the parts that they have the same intention. Ask what resources each has that the other would like.

7. Now remind the parts that they were once part of a larger whole. Imagine that they are sharing these resources now – you may see this, or feel it or hear it in your mind's eye.

8. Bring your hands together and as you do this, allow the parts to integrate. Bring the integrated image inside your body by symbolically placing your hands on your chest. You may feel or see or hear something as you do this.

9. Future pace: Imagine a future situation where in the past there was conflict. What will be different this time?

DISCOVER STRATEGIES FOR SUCCESS

All your everyday behaviour is determined by your strategies. A strategy is the order in which you do things to produce a result. You have different strategies for love, learning, motivation, being convinced and making decisions. This chapter looks at how to change your strategies in order to produce a new outcome.

STRATEGIES

How aware are you of the strategies you use to decide when to fall in love, what to eat and drink or what to buy? Were you even aware that you had strategies for these things? A strategy is the 'way' you do something – the order and sequence that produces an outcome. When you change a strategy you can produce a different outcome.

Many of the strategies we use to get different results are entirely unconscious. NLP is concerned with how your strategies work, how you can change them to produce different results and how you can master strategies of excellence. It is like a recipe for the brain. You take different ingredients (or experiences) and decide how to put them together. Which ingredients you choose and how you put them together will determine whether you end up with cake or steak.

Types of strategy

There are many different types of strategy. Some of the key strategies you may want to discover are your learning, decision-making, motivation, buying, deep love and problem strategies. If these are working well for you, then that's obviously fine. However, there may be some that you wish to change.

Learning strategy. This provides the means by which you pick up and retain new information. You may have different learning strategies for different subjects.

Decision-making strategy. These strategies govern how you come up with a decision. Some people have decision-making strategies that are so complex that they rarely reach the point of making a decision. If you belong in this category, you need to examine your strategies.

Motivation strategy. These are the means by which you get yourself to do something. If you don't find it easy to start or complete tasks, take a look at your motivation strategies.

Buying strategy. If you are in business, it is essential to understand your customers' buying strategies. How they make the decision unconsciously may be very different from the reasons they give you out loud.

How do you decide to buy something in your personal life? If you have a large credit bill and a lot of possessions you don't really need, your buying strategy may not be working for you. You need to change it so that you are spending within your means, not following your shopping impulses.

Deep love strategy. Do you know how you know that you are in love with someone or that you are deeply loved by someone? It may be useful to understand your own and your partner's deep love strategy.

Problem strategy. Have you ever met someone who is always complaining about the number of problems that he has. A problem is simply an outcome that a person doesn't want. 'Chunk down' (see pp.114-16). Get specific and identify what results that person is getting that he no longer wants. For each problem, check the strategy – find out how he is producing the result. Once you know the strategy you can change it.

Smoking, drinking, overeating. If you produce a specific action that is a problem for you, for example smoking, eating or drinking too much, you can change your strategies and lose the problem.

Using strategies

As we have seen, experiences are stored in the brain using the five sensory representational systems. They are refined by the submodalities in which they are stored. In addition, they are stored with reference to the order in which they occur – a strategy. Every sequence of stored experiences leads to an outcome.

You do things externally – behave – in an order. You also think internally in an order. Both are strategies. All your external behaviour is also controlled by an internal strategy. If a strategy is repeated exactly in the way and order it occurs, it will produce the same results. If you change it – either internally or externally – it will produce a different result.

One reason you may want to learn more about your strategies is that if they are not getting you the results you want, you can change them – not just to get different results but also to get truly excellent results.

If you want to learn to be successful at something, look for a person who is a master at it. Replicate their strategy and you can become a master at it too. Changing your strategies using the techniques of NLP produces on-going, generative change.

THE TOTE MODEL

There are several models you can use to discover your own and other people's strategies. The TOTE model is the most commonly used NLP model for analysing someone's unconscious strategies.

The TOTE model comes from the work of George Miller, Eugene Galanter and Karl Pribram and was outlined in their book *Plans and the Structure of Behaviour* (see p. 186). Every strategy you run can be broken down according to this model. The TOTE model lays out the route between where you are now (the present state) and an end state – how you go from the starting point of not doing something to the place where you do it.

The TOTE model consists of four parts that generally happen very quickly and outside your conscious awareness. Before using the TOTE model, decide what strategy you are looking at.

1. Test (T)
In the first test you compare where you are now (the present state) with where you want to be (your outcome or desired state). If there is a gap between the two, then something needs to happen for you to get what you want. For example,

you want to make a decision. The test stage shows
that you haven't decided yet.

2. Operate (O)

In order to reach the desired state (in this case
a decision), you take an action. This is a data-
gathering stage. You might evaluate lots of
different data and come up with several actions
that you could take.

To find out how another person does this stage, ask
them questions about what they do, in what order,
and if any step doesn't work, what they do next.
(The questions to ask are given in the 5-minute
exercises on pp. 166-9.)

Some actions are very simple, but others are more
complex and may be made up of more than one
TOTE. If you have a lot of choice at the operate
stage, then you are more likely to be able to move
from your present state to your desired state.

3. Test (T)

The second test checks whether you have taken an
action or several actions that are sufficient to allow
the gap between the present stage and desired
state to disappear. For example, have you

unconsciously gathered enough information to allow yourself to decide now?

4. Exit (E)
If the answer is 'yes', then the outcome is achieved and the strategy exits or completes. In this case, a decision is made. If the answer is 'no', then the strategy can't exit and you find yourself unable to come to a decision.

5-minute exercise: eliciting someone's learning strategy
1. Ask the person to think of a time when he could learn something easily and rapidly.
2. Then ask him:
Test: 'How do you know it is time to begin learning?'
Operation: 'What do you do in order to learn?'
Test: 'How do you know if you have learned something?'
Exit: 'What lets you know that you have learned something fully?'

5-minute exercise: eliciting someone's love strategy
To make your relationship secure, satisfy your partner's love strategy as well as your own.

1. To elicit your partner's love strategy, first of all ask him: 'How do you know when you are totally loved by someone else?'
2. 'Or can you remember a specific time when you were totally loved?'
3. 'In order to know you are totally loved, is it necessary for you:
• to be taken to places and bought things?
• to be looked at with that special look?
• to hear that special tone of voice or those special words?
• to be touched in a certain way or a certain part of your body?'
4. Pay attention to the main sense they refer to and any steps in their strategy.

Extended exercise: eliciting an unconscious strategy

If you are working with another person and need to find out (elicit) their strategies, you can use the following technique:
1. Get into rapport with the other person (see pp. 66–8).
2. Now get into the state you want to elicit, since this will help him to get into the right state too.

3. Ensure he is associated into the state in the situation you want to ask him about by asking him questions which take him to that time, for example:

'Can you recall a time when you were totally motivated/in love/learning well?'

'Can you recall a specific time?'

'As you go back to that time now…what was the very first thing that caused you to be totally motivated/in love/learning well?'

'Was it something you saw? Was it the way someone looked at you?'

'Was it something you heard? Was it someone's tone of voice?'

'Was it the touch of someone or something?'

'What was the very first thing that caused you to be totally motivated/in love/learning well?'

4. He may come up with an answer that is visual, kinaesthetic or auditory. Ask him for the next step in the sequence.

'After you saw/heard/felt that, what happened next?'

'Did you picture something in your mind?'

'Did you say something to yourself?'

'Did you have a certain feeling or emotion?'

'What happened next?'

'After you did that, did you know that you were totally motivated/in love/learning well?'

5. Check you have a logical sequence of steps.
6. Check that you have the key pieces of the strategy – the beginning, middle and the end.

WRITING DOWN A STRATEGY

It is useful to write down a strategy so that you can refer back to it when you need to modify it or use it again.

The strategies in NLP are often written down as abbreviations to signify the representational system used at each stage:

Visual is written as **V**
Auditory as **A**
Kinaesthetic as **K**
Olfactory as **O**
Gustatory as **G**

An additional set of abbreviations signify whether it is remembered (^{r}) or constructed (^{c}), and external (^{e}) or internal (^{i}).

For example, something you hear inside your head would be written A^i. If you remember an image it would be written V^r. Self-talk, or auditory dialogue, is written A^{id} (auditory internal digital). All strategies exit with an internal feeling: K^i.

AN EXAMPLE OF A BUYING STRATEGY

A man sees a shirt in a shop and thinks 'That looks interesting.' He touches the shirt to feel its texture, then asks the shop assistant how much it is and decides to buy it. He leaves feeling good.

This strategy would be written as:`
V^e (visual external)
A^{id} (auditory internal digital)
K^e (kinaesthetic external)
A^e (auditory external)
K^i (kinaesthetic internal)

USING METAPHORS

A metaphor in NLP is any story used to illustrate a point or idea. Storytelling is an age-old tool used to connect with both the conscious and the unconscious and impart wisdom. The listener identifies with a key character, which helps them to accept the message of the story. You can use metaphors to increase the effectiveness of your communication with other people, especially with their unconscious mind. While facts and explanations may cause your mind to wander from the subject, stories are easy for the unconscious mind to remember.

Metaphors can highlight hopes, beliefs, anxieties and solutions. They can help in a situation where if you were to speak about those ideas directly, the listener might be consciously resistant.

Metaphors have been used throughout history. The great philosophers and teachers all used stories in order to simplify the ideas they were teaching. For example, fairy stories are metaphors that have long been used to demonstrate a point about change and transition. Think about *Cinderella* or *The Ugly Duckling*. It does not matter that they are about a fantasy character, we still identify with their transformation.

HOW TO USE METAPHORS

1. Choose a metaphor that your listener can relate to and that is appropriate in the context you are using it.
2. Use the metaphor to establish rapport. Storytelling is fun.
3. Relate each feature of the idea you are selling to a feature in the story.
4. Use language of the representational system that your listener will most relate to.
5. Keep the language positive. Always create a positive internal representation inside the listener's head as you move him within the story to your goal. Avoid clichés.
6. You can also use embedded quotes. Have one person say something to another in the story in quotes (for example, 'Just pay attention to what I have to say.'). The listener will feel that he is being addressed directly without finding the statement confrontational.
7. If you think the listener has a question about the idea that you are expressing, actually include that question in the story (perhaps asked by a character) and then answer it in the story as well.

A metaphor is a wonderful way to bypass the conscious mind and to help another person to invent their own solutions for change. The best stories will capture the imagination and provoke the listener to look at a situation afresh or do something that he might not otherwise attempt.

What does the metaphor mean for you?
At first, a metaphor may appear to hold no relevance for your life, but after a while, you realize that the characters, images and words are starting to mean something to you. Even if you don't realize that straightaway, your unconscious enjoys working out what the story might mean for you, and that in itself can bring new realizations.

How a metaphor is heard
Metaphors engage the right brain in the same way as dreams, because they are symbolic and entertain as well as inform. The listener takes from the metaphor what he wants to take unconsciously and applies it to his own situation. Resistance to accepting the message is decreased because a story is much less confrontational than a direct statement addressed to the conscious mind. Within the content of the story you can present different points of view, suggest actions and propose solutions, and elicit any number of states – it provides sufficient scope to reframe the listener taking him from a negative state to an intermediate then a positive state. Just think how

METAPHOR EXAMPLE:
THE STORY OF THE WISEST MAN

A king once wanted to find the wisest man in the kingdom to be his prime minister. His courtiers told him there were three such men.

The king called all three to his palace and set them a test. He shut them in the same room and told them that they had been locked in with the most complex lock ever devised. Whoever could open the lock first would be appointed head of his government.

Two of the wise men immediately began to calculate the combination of the lock using the most advanced mathematics. Meanwhile, the third sat and did nothing but think quietly. Then, after a little while, he walked over to the door and put his hand on the handle. The unlocked door opened immediately...

useful that would be with a person who does not find it easy to make up his mind or gets stuck in one state and finds it impossible to move on.

Metaphors from personal experience

Stories are examples of metaphors that draw on archetypal images. The second type of metaphor is described by the therapist David Grove and has been extensively developed by Penny Tomkins and James Lawley. These type of metaphors draw from personal experience.

You can work out someone's personal metaphors by listening to what he says. They may just be a turn of phrase, an expression, an image that keeps coming to mind or even a memory: it doesn't matter. They describe a real internal experience that the person has. The metaphor shows how he has stored this experience in sensory terms, be it visual, auditory, kinaesthetic, gustatory or olfactory.

Personal metaphors contain lots of valuable information about how the person perceives and thinks about the world. This information is revealed in symbolic form in the words he uses. Listen for both overt and implied metaphors in a person's speech. Any metaphor a person uses will have a special significance for him.

Personal metaphors can explain a lot. Suppose someone says, 'I feel a knot in my stomach every time I get anxious.' You can uncover the personal significance, function and attributes the person has given to this knot. Using his language, get him to describe the metaphor:

- ✓ What does it look like? How big/thick is it? What is it made of?
- ✓ Where is it? Symbols are stored in precise locations.
- ✓ Is there a time sequence? The order of events in a person's internal metaphorical landscape is important.

Suppose he answers: 'The knot is brown with black bits, quite large, as if it has taken over my whole stomach.' Straight away you have more words and images to work with. 'Taken over?' 'What's that like to you?' 'Is it a knot that is hard or one that is soft and pliable?' One person might see the knot as acting like a shield, while another person sees it as preventing some action and yet another as absorbing an emotion.

PERSONAL METAPHORS

Overt metaphors:

'I keep hitting my head against a brick wall.'

'He broke my heart.'

'You look down in the dumps.'

Implied metaphors:

'Stop running away from the argument.'

'I am feeling under enormous pressure here.'

'I feel I can't get through to him.'

PUTTING IT ALL TOGETHER

This final section looks at ways in which you can bring together the techniques of NLP in a systematic way to create better results in any area of your life.

You can use NLP to help yourself, personally, professionally and socially, and also to help or coach someone else. Because NLP is about modelling excellence, you can use it in any situation where you want to learn how someone does something well.

When you want a new result, first remember to clarify where you are now (your present state), your values and beliefs. Then write down an outcome (your desired state). Next, identify what blocks you need to overcome and what actions you need to create your outcome.

WHEN TO USE DIFFERENT NLP TECHNIQUES

Anchors (see pp. 127-37): to move from a negative to a positive state, including depression (stacking and chaining anchors as well as resource anchoring)

Association (see pp. 44-5): to have (or get someone to have) a 'real' experience of something

Belief change (see pp. 143-4): to resolve an unconscious conflict that is stopping the achievement of an outcome; to deal with fears and limits

Disney Method (see pp. 87-9): to produce creative thinking and an achievable vision

Dissociation (see pp. 44-5): to get rid of over-involvement

Logical levels (see pp. 139-43): to check the alignment of change throughout all neurological levels

Matching (see pp. 70-3): to gain rapport in personal or business relationships, especially in presentations, meetings, negotiation and selling

Mental rehearsal (see p. 83): to future pace a situation to create change or see how effective change has been

Meta Model (see pp. 92-100): to challenge thinking and move from a state of 'stuckness'

Metaphors (see pp. 171-6): to loosen up thinking and produce a new state or unconscious change

Milton Model (see pp. 100-13): to create trance

Outcomes (see pp. 76-87): to get clear on aims and how to achieve them

Parts integration technique (see pp. 157-9): to address self-sabotage and conflicts in outcomes

Perceptual positions (see pp. 116-19): to change a viewpoint about a relationship

Phobia process (see pp. 151-3): to resolve phobias

Rapport (see pp. 66-8): when using techniques with others

Reframing (see pp. 123-6): to change an outlook or viewpoint
Swish pattern (see pp. 149-51): to change a habit
Values, changing (see pp. 155-7): to resolve an unconscious conflict that is blocking an outcome

USING NLP TECHNIQUES FOR YOURSELF

NLP techniques can be used to produce change on many levels. Simple techniques such as reframing, perceptual positions and future pacing shake up your thinking so you see a situation differently. Anchoring, too, will result in a quick change by producing more resourceful states. If you want to stop biting your nails or eat less chocolate, a swish pattern will help you.

However, sometimes you need to use more than one technique. For example, to resolve low self-esteem, forge better relationships, lose weight or discover why you keep getting into debt, you may need to discover what is going on beneath the surface and to use a combination of some techniques. These might include values and belief changes, strategies and metaphors.

Finally, you may want to gain new resources and/or learn a new skill. If so, the quickest way may be to find a model of excellence and learn his strategies for success.

The modelling process

When you model a person, you work out how he does what he does well – makes money, communicates, or plays tennis, for instance – and how you can replicate it. In fact, you can model any strategy.

1. Find the best person to model, otherwise you will simply adopt the flaws inherent in the behaviour you are modelling.
2. If you are talking about a large subject – running a successful business, for instance – break down what he does into component parts (how the firm sells, manages staff and clients, etc). It may be useful to start with the smallest and easiest component.
3. Look at the following:

✓ **Observe the person's physiology** How does he stand, sit or move? Pay attention to his posture as well as his breathing.

✓ **Why does he do what he does?** What provides the motivation for the consistent results he gets?

✓ **What are his filter patterns?** If you can ask him directly, do so. Otherwise, work them out by observing his behaviour and listening to what he says. What are his Meta programmes, values and core beliefs with regard to what you want to model? Why does he behave in the way that he does?

✓ **Strategies** Observe the strategies he uses such as the order and sequence in which he does things, or elicit his internal strategies (see pp. 167-9) to find out what produces his behaviour.

✓ **Feedback** How does he get feedback on his progress and success?

✓ **Discover what is critical** to obtaining the end result.

✓ **Test your theory** by dropping different elements until you determine what is essential and what is not.

✓ **Do it yourself** Adopt his ways of thinking, do things for the same reason and replicate his actions. If you don't get the same results consistently, what have you missed?

✓ **Teach someone else** If you do get the same results consistently, you have successfully modelled a strategy for success, and you can show others how to get them as well.

USING NLP TECHNIQUES WITH OTHERS

When you are coaching another person it is vital to ensure that he takes responsibility for the results he gets. How motivated is he to change? It is that person, not you, who will be making the changes.

You are simply giving him the techniques to do so. Remind him upfront of the cause/effect equation. For every effect there is a cause. As he has created the results that he has in his life right now, he is responsible for his future results too. Not you.

Introduce him to the core beliefs or presuppositions of NLP, especially 'People already have all the resources they need.' Make it clear that you are not a therapist or a doctor. You can simply help someone to discover and use his own resources through the NLP techniques.

Part one: preparation
1. First check your state and your congruency. Whenever you use NLP techniques with another person, make sure that you are in a positive state and believe that you and the other person are able to get the positive result that he wants.
2. Create rapport. Use the rapport-building skills that have been outlined in Forming relationships (see pp. 66-8) – for example, calibration, matching and mirroring.
3. What is that person's outcome? Why is he here? What is the issue he wants to resolve? What is the result he is getting? What does he want instead? Introduce the person to the beliefs of NLP.

4. Map his existing model of the world. Use the Meta Model to gather information about his model of the world. Notice the representational systems he uses, his Meta programmes, beliefs and values.

5. What needs to change? Notice what resources he has already to get his outcome. What limits him? What needs to change? Pay attention to any belief or value conflicts and strategies that are not effective, and to any core issues relating to his outcome – what is the difference that will make the most difference?

Part two: creating change

6. The first step to create change is to loosen the person's model of the world, i.e. shake up the certainty of his thinking. Use the Milton Model, Meta Model, chunking, perceptual positions and reframing to show the person what he is currently deleting, distorting, generalizing and filtering.

7. Create change and build resources. Depending on the situation, you may want to use just one technique or several. How can you help the person to resolve any conflicts, remove blocks and build his existing resources? Use anchoring, reframing, swish patterns, belief and values changes or strategy changes. Check for alignment with the Logical Levels model.

Part three: check

8. Test the result. Check whether or not the techniques you have used have been successful. Observe (calibrate for) changes in his language and physiology. Elicit beliefs and values to check how the person has changed. Notice if there has been any change in his representational system. If there are any incongruencies, you may need to use the parts integration technique.

9. Future pace. Check that the result will be ongoing. What new behaviour will the person be exhibiting in the future? Are they convinced by the change? The simplest way to do this is to get him to imagine himself at a specific time in the future. Use associated and dissociated mental rehearsal (see pp. 44-5). A three-month time frame works well enough to convince many people, though you may want to go much further if he is very big picture in his thinking or to ask him to imagine several points in the future. When he is there, ask him what he sees, hears and feels. Is he on the way to achieving the result he asked for?

As you use the NLP techniques with others, keep in mind the idea of 'experimentation'. Have fun and try things. Be flexible and you will get the result you want.

FURTHER READING

Harry Adler, NLP: The New Art and Science of Getting What You Want, Piatkus Books 1994

Steve and Connirae Andreas, Change Your Mind and Keep the Change, Real People Press 1988

Steve and Connirae Andreas, Core Transformation, Real People Press 1996

Steve Andreas and Charles Faulkner, NLP: The Technology of Achievement, Nicholas Brealey Publishing Ltd 1996

Richard Bandler, Using Your Brain for a Change, Real People Press 1985

Richard Bandler and John Grinder, Frogs into Princes, Real People Press 1981

Richard Bandler and John Grinder, The Structure of Magic: A Book About Language and Therapy, v. I, Science and Behaviour Books 1989

Michael Brooks, Instant Rapport, Time Warner International 1990

Robert Dilts, Changing Belief Systems with NLP, Meta Publications, 1990

Robert Dilts, Visionary Leadership Skills, Meta Publications, 1996

Robert Dilts, Tim Hallborn and Suzie Smith, Beliefs, Metamorphous Press 1990

David Gordon, Therapeutic Metaphors: Helping Others Through the Looking Glass, Gordon Meta Publications 1989

Sue Knight, NLP at Work: The Difference that Makes

a Difference in Business, Nicholas Brealey Publishing Ltd 2002

Tad James and Wyatt Woodsmall, *Time Line Therapy and the Basis of Personality*, Meta Publications 1989

Michael McMaster and John Grinder, *Precision: New Approach to Communication*, Metamorphous Press 1994

George Miller, Eugene Galanter and Karl Pribam, *Plans and the Structure of Behaviour*, Holt, R&W 1969

Joseph O'Connor and John Seymour, *Introducing NLP*, HarperCollins 2003

John Overdurf and Julie Silverthorn, *Training Trances*, Metamorphous Press 1995

Anthony Robbins, *Unlimited Power*, Pocket Books 2001

Anthony Robbins, *Awaken the Giant Within*, Pocket Books 1993

Michael Talbot, *The Holographic Universe*, HarperCollins 1996

David Shepherd and Tad James, *Presenting Magically: Transforming Your Stage Presence with NLP*, Crown House

USEFUL WEBSITES

http://www.nlpuniversitypress.com/indexR.html
Online NLP encyclopedia

http://www.cleanlanguage.co.uk/ Symbolic modelling, clean language, the metaphor therapy of David Grove

www.davidgrove.com
The metaphor therapy of David Grove

GLOSSARY

Accessing cues The movements that show how a person is thinking and processing information inside themselves. They include eye movements, gestures, breathing and changes in posture.

Align To co-ordinate or arrange so that all steps and parts of a process are moving towards the same outcome.

Anchor An external stimulus or trigger that sets off an internal response. Can be visual, auditory or kinaesthetic.

Behavioural flexibility Having the ability to change your ways of doing things and being around other people in order to get the outcome or response you want from them.

Break state Doing something that quickly changes the focus of your attention and your state.

Calibration/to calibrate The ability to observe what is going on with another person through reading their non-verbal signals.

Chaining anchors Changing someone's emotional state by setting up a series of anchors that they move through one by one to move from the present state to a desired state.

Chunking Gaining a different viewpoint by looking at a situation from a different level. To chunk, you can move up, down or sideways.

Congruence When your outcome is fully aligned with your beliefs, values, identity, etc. and when your verbal communication is aligned with your non-verbal communication.

Context reframe Giving a new perspective and meaning to something by changing the context.

Dissociated A state of being outside an experience rather than looking at it through your own eyes.

Distortion An internal representation that is changed in some way.

Eye movements/accessing cues Changes in the directions in which the eyes move when thinking in the visual, auditory and kinaesthetic systems and imagining or remembering.

Frame A particular way of looking at something. By changing the frame you can change the meaning.

Future pacing Mentally rehearsing/trying on an experience in the future as if it is happening to you now in order to get the desired behaviour to occur naturally and unconsciously.

Generalization The process by which one part of your experience is changed to become a class of experience.

Incongruence Lack of congruence and alignment leading to blocks and internal conflict in realizing an outcome.

Intention The conscious or unconscious purpose of behaviour.

Internal representation How you store information in your mind in terms of pictures, sounds, tastes, smells and feelings – sensory modalities.

Lead representational system The system you use to access your internal information.

Logical levels A model of environment, behaviour, capability, belief, identity and spirituality.

Meta Model A set of questions and language patterns designed to uncover deletion, generalization and distortion and to give additional resources.

Meta programme The unconscious programming we all have on a mental level that decides how we filter and chunk experience.

Milton Model The model of language patterns based on the speech and techniques of hypnotherapist Milton Erickson. It uses deliberately vague language to communicate with the unconscious.

Modal operators Language patterns to do with possibility or necessity, for example 'may', 'can'.

Modelling Analyzing how something works systematically and breaking it down into a usable model that can be replicated by other people to achieve a desired outcome.

Outcome A goal, result or desired state that has been defined in specific terms to do with seeing, feeling or hearing.

Pacing Matching another person's behaviour and thinking to achieve or maintain rapport.

Predicate A word that indicates that a person is relating to a particular representational system.

Preferred representational system The representational system a person uses as a matter of preference.

Presuppositions The core beliefs that NLP has adopted as useful beliefs.

Rapport A state in which two people feel a sense of trust and relationship with one another.

Reframing Putting a different frame on an experience in order to give it a positive meaning.

Strategy A sequence of thoughts that leads to an outcome.

Submodalities The small distinctions in how a particular sensory experience is coded internally, for example a picture can be bright or dark.

Swish pattern A generative technique for changing habits or limiting behaviour.

TOTE Test, Operate, Test, Exit – the sequence that describes the structure of a strategy. The basis for producing any behaviour.

Trance A state of relaxation in which communication with the unconscious is facilitated.

Values hierarchy The order of what is important to you.

INDEX